W9-AJC-871

THE LittleHands Nature Book

Nancy Fusco Castaldo

illustrations by Loretta Trezzo Braren

WILLIAMSON PUBLISHING • CHARLOTTE, VERMONT

Library of Congress
Cataloging-in-Publication Data
Fusco Castaldo, Nancy, 1962–
   [Sunny days & starry nights]
   The little hands nature book: earth, sky,
critters & more / Nancy Fusco Castaldo;
illustrations by Loretta Trezzo Braren.
      p. cm.—(A Williamson little hands book)
   Previously published as: Sunny days & starry
nights.
   Includes index.
   Summary: Explores the outdoors and teaches
about a variety of plants and animals with over
sixty suggested activities.
   ISBN 1-885593-16-3
   1. Nature study—Juvenile literature.
2. Natural history—Outdoor books—Juvenile
literature. 3. Early childhood education—
Activity programs—Juvenile literature.
[1. Nature study. 2. Natural history.]
I. Braren, Loretta Trezzo, ill.   II. Title.
III. Series.
LB1139.5.S35F87   1997
372.3'57—dc21   97-13774
                                  CIP
                                  AC

Cover design: Trezzo-Braren Studio
Interior design: Trezzo-Braren Studio
Illustrations: Loretta Trezzo Braren
Printing: Capital City Press

Williamson Publishing Co.
P.O. Box 185
Charlotte, Vermont 05445
1-800-234-8791

Manufactured in the United States of America
10 9 8 7 6 5 4

CONTENTS

For Lucie, who helps me share in the wonderment.

♥

My heartfelt thanks to:
My husband, Dean, for inspiring and supporting my dreams,
My parents, for showing me the beauty of nature,
My family and friends, for their readiness to listen and
constant support.

♥

A special thanks to Susan and Jack Williamson
for believing in my dream.

STEPPING STONES

★ A WORD TO GROWN-UPS

Some of the most wonderful childhood experiences occur outdoors. Early picnics on warm summer mornings, splashing in the waves at the seashore, taking a walk in the rain, watching fireflies twinkle in the twilight, and forming snowballs on a cold winter's day are a child's first experiences in the natural world.

The Little Hands Nature Book was written to enhance these experiences and offer additional activities to further creative exploration of the world we all share. Although geared for children between the ages of two and six, older children will be able to take the projects one step further and will need less supervision. It is recommended, though, that even older children be escorted into wooded areas or when playing in water — even in a wading pool.

These experiences and activities are meant to serve as stepping stones to outdoor exploration. One of the most wonderful things about nature is that it is full of surprises. It is because of this that most of the activities can be explored over and over again, each time creating a different outcome and learning experience. These projects have been purposefully selected to enhance children's creativity, observational skills, and understanding of their natural world.

PRACTICAL MATTERS FOR NATURE LOVERS

Before starting out on any outdoor adventure become familiar with your surroundings. For a safe experience, visit nature preserves and parks. Keep in mind that looking closely in your own backyard — no matter how tiny — can be a great sunny day or starry night experience. The deep woods are not necessary or even desirable for very young children. Whether you are taking your own child or a small group of children, outdoor exploration — even in your own backyard — begs a few precautions. Be aware of any particular concerns in your area, be it Lyme disease, rabies, or hunting seasons. Your local Cooperative Extension can provide you with most information.

Wear sensible clothes for the outdoors, including sturdy shoes and long pants. Sunscreen and a hat should complete any outdoor attire in summer. Children love to collect things, so encourage collecting where possible. Many items such as pebbles, colored leaves, and seeds are expendable even in wildlife sanctuaries, but let children observe you asking permission before collecting anything. On the other hand, wildflowers are often off limits for picking, so bring the experience to life by drawing flowers or talking about their colors, shapes, and sizes. There is lots more to take away from an outdoor experience than the flowers or rocks themselves.

Discourage children from disturbing natural habitats and "adopting" living wildlife for pets. An important aspect of every venture outdoors is to learn to respect and to protect every living thing.

Children should be taught early on not to venture into the woods alone and never to wander away from their group. As a good example, let the children hear you tell someone where you are going and when you expect to return.

Most of all, have fun. Enjoy the time spent together collecting memories and experiences!

EXPLORING THE OUTDOORS

Take out your hand lens and get ready for a wild adventure!

A TEENY, TINY HIKE

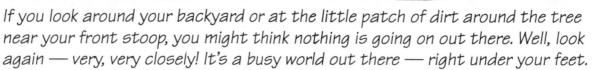

If you look around your backyard or at the little patch of dirt around the tree near your front stoop, you might think nothing is going on out there. Well, look again — very, very closely! It's a busy world out there — right under your feet.

HERE'S WHAT YOU NEED

Hand lens

4 stones

HERE'S WHAT YOU DO

1 With a helper, mark the corners of a small area with the stones. Hike the ground on your hands and knees — creeping, crawling, lying down, looking up. What does the area feel like? Grassy or rocky? Cool or warm?

2 Explore the area with your hand lens. Do you see any insects? Do they have wings or lots of feet? Are there any signs that people or bigger animals were in your area?

3 Make three observations about what you see, such as "I see a ladybug walking up a small blade of grass."

MORE NATURE FUN!

☆ Some other insects you might see include ants, crickets, leaf hoppers, and worms. Which critters move by *jumping, hopping, crawling, slithering,* or *scampering*?

☆ After your field trip, draw two pictures of something you saw. Draw one picture from *far away* (standing up) and one picture of the same thing *close up* (as seen through a hand lens).

☆ Plan to take another hike when the season changes. What do you think will look the *same* and what will look *different*?

☆ Read *One Small Square Backyard* by Donald M. Silver for fun facts.

SOW BUG

PILL BUG

ANT

GRASSHOPPER

WORM

WISE OWL

Armored Bugs

You might have been lucky to find a sow bug or pill bug on your hike. They are tiny insects about the size of your fingernail with many legs. Sow bugs and pill bugs look like they are wearing a suit of armor. Some of them can even roll up into a tiny ball to protect themselves when picked up. Sow bugs and pill bugs have 7 pairs of legs. Both are oval, dark, about 1/2 inch (1 cm). Pills roll up very tightly; sow bugs not as tightly — that's the only difference.

WINDOW-ON-THE-WORLD

Make your very own window-on-the-world nature notebook to write in and draw about what you **observe**, or see, from your window. Your nature notebook will be your personal record of what is happening around you.

HERE'S WHAT YOU NEED

Loose-leaf binder with unlined paper

Pencils, markers, and crayons

Old magazines and safety scissors (optional)

HERE'S WHAT YOU DO

1 Draw the different birds that come to your feeder or draw the shape of the moon every night for a month, or keep track of the weather every Saturday for a whole year!

2 Cut pictures out of magazines of favorite animals or flowers that you see to glue into your notebook.

SPRING

MARCH 21:
I SAW NEW PLANTS BEGIN TO GROW.

MARCH 22:
A ROBIN ATE AT THE BIRD FEEDER.

SUMMER

JUNE 21:
A PRETTY BUTTERFLY SAT ON A FLOWER.

JUNE 22:
I FOUND SOME SEA SHELLS.

FALL

SEPTEMBER 23:
THE LEAVES ARE TURNING RED, YELLOW, AND BROWN.

SEPTEMBER 24:
APPLES ARE FALLING FROM OUR APPLE TREE. YUMMY!

WINTER

DECEMBER 22:
IT IS SNOWING!

DECEMBER 23:
THE TEMPERATURE IS 20 DEGREES.

MORE NATURE FUN!

☆ Make sure to date all of your notebook pages. It will be fun to look at the book each season and see what has changed right outside your window.

☆ Read *Window* by Jeannie Baker to see the changes that occur outside one window over the years.

☆ Draw what you see outside of your window each season. Draw the windowpanes and then the outdoors — just the way you see them!

☆ Ask a friend to read you *Winnie-the-Pooh* by A.A. Milne ("In Which Piglet Is Entirely Surrounded by Water," Chapter IX) about Christopher Robin's experience watching rain on his window.

NATURE BINGO

As you find each of the nature objects on your homemade, nature bingo board, check it off with a marker. Make sure to yell NATURE when all of the objects in a row are found.

HERE'S WHAT YOU NEED

Construction paper

Markers

Ruler

FOLD PAPER INTO THIRDS LENGTHWISE. DRAW LINES; FOLD WIDTHWISE; DRAW LINES ON FOLDS

FOLDS

DRAW A NATURE OBJECT IN EACH SQUARE

CONSTRUCTION PAPER

HERE'S WHAT YOU DO

1 Fold your paper into thirds. Using the ruler, draw straight lines on the folds.

2 Turn the paper around and fold the paper into thirds again. Draw lines on the new folds, too. Your paper should now have three rows of three squares.

3 In each square draw something to look for in nature, such as a tree, nest, flower, puddle, insect, frog, pinecone, leaf, or acorn.

4 When you have drawn a picture in each square, you are ready to play Nature Bingo!

MORE NATURE FUN!

☆ Play Nature Bingo in your backyard, on a walk through a park, looking out your car window, or when browsing through a picture encyclopedia.

☆ Let's get down to details! Instead of looking for any flower, cloud, bird, and leaf, look for a *yellow* flower, *dark* cloud, *red* bird, and *hand-shaped* leaf.

☆ Go for the gold — play Super Nature Bingo! See if you can be the first to check off every square on your Nature Bingo game board.

TRUE OR FALSE?

Have fun playing Simon Says, "True or False?" with at least one other person. Just like in regular Simon Says, the secret is to listen carefully before copying Simon.

HERE'S WHAT YOU DO

1 Choose one person to be Simon.

2 Simon will say a sentence about nature. If the sentence is true, repeat it back to Simon. If the sentence is not true, don't say anything.

3 Take turns being Simon. See how many nature facts you can stump your friends with.

MORE NATURE FUN!

☆ Practice with these nature sentences. Do you know which one is not true?

Trees have leaves.

Birds have feathers.

Feathers help birds fly.

Birds give us milk.

If you did not repeat the last sentence after Simon, you are right. (Birds do not give us milk. Cows and goats give us milk.)

☆ Riddles often tell some interesting facts about something and ask you to guess what it is. Read *The Wackiest Nature Riddles on Earth* by Mike Artell for some fun animal riddles, and then make up your own.

Birds of a Feather

Did you know that there are some birds that are not able to fly? Amazing, but true, ostriches, emus, kiwis, and penguins don't fly, even though they have wings and feathers.

SHADOW PICTURES

Do you remember when Peter Pan asks Wendy to sew his shadow back onto his feet? Well, shadows aren't really attached to your feet, of course, but they sure do seem to "stick" to you on a sunny day!

HERE'S WHAT YOU NEED

1 large sheet of newsprint or poster board

Markers or crayons

Leaf

HERE'S WHAT YOU DO

1 Place the paper on the ground in direct sunlight.

2 Ask a friend to hold the leaf, so that its shadow falls on the paper.

3 Trace the leaf's shadow with a marker. Then, lay the leaf down next to your drawing. Is the leaf larger or smaller than the shadow picture?

4 Leave the paper in the same place. Hold up the leaf and draw the picture again later in the day. In the second shadow picture, does the shadow get *larger, smaller,* or stay the *same size*?

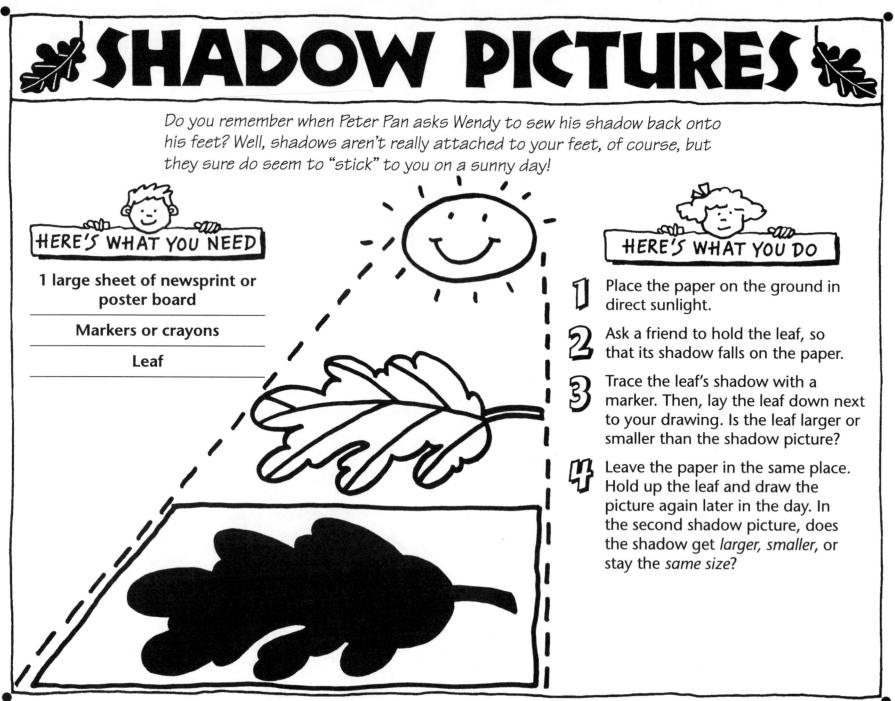

MORE NATURE FUN!

☆ Do a shadow dance. Put on some music that suits your feelings — slow and graceful like a tree bending in the wind or jazzy and fast like a squirrel hiding its nuts. Now dance with your shadow to the beat! Does your shadow do exactly the same thing that you do?

☆ Do you ever feel lonely? Most of us do. Next time you feel all alone, put on a sun hat and some sunscreen, grab your favorite picture book, sit in the sun, and look at your book — together with your shadow!

MAKE-A-SUNDIAL

By exploring shadows on a sunny day, we can even tell time — just like people did long ago. The only problem with shadow clocks is that you can't use them on a cloudy day or at night!

HERE'S WHAT YOU NEED

Paper plate

8-inch (20 cm) stick or straw

Crayons

Ruler

MORE NATURE FUN!

☆ Try making shadows at night with a flashlight. Shine the light on the wall. Place your hand in front of the light. Can you make your hand look like an animal? The sun creates shadows exactly the same way. A tree, person, or building is like the hand and the sun is like the flashlight.

HERE'S WHAT YOU DO

1 Draw a happy face on the plate and color it.

2 Bring the plate outside on a sunny day and place it on the ground. Poke the stick through the middle of the plate.

3 Now, draw a line from the stick to the outside of the plate with the ruler. Slant the stick towards the line and the outside of the plate.

4 When it is noon (1:00 P.M. if you are on daylight-saving time), turn the plate so that the shadow of the stick falls along the line you drew. Ask a grown-up to fasten your plate to the ground with tacks. Each hour, check the position of the shadow along the edge of the plate; mark it and have a grown-up write in the time beside it. Draw lines from the stick to the marks. On the next sunny day you will be able to tell the time by watching where the shadow falls on your sundial.

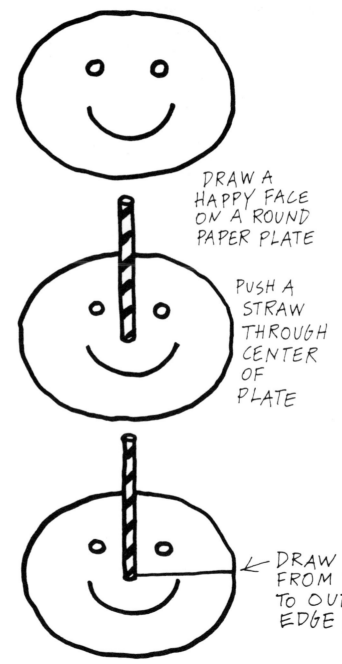

DRAW A HAPPY FACE ON A ROUND PAPER PLATE

PUSH A STRAW THROUGH CENTER OF PLATE

DRAW A LINE FROM STRAW TO OUTSIDE EDGE OF PLATE

WISE OWL

Me and My Shadow

Shadows are caused by the movement of the sun across the sky. The sun rises each morning in the east and sets each night in the west. The mid-day sun is directly overhead, which is when shadows are shortest. Is there any time on a sunny day when you don't have a shadow? Can you make your shadow disappear? Can you make it touch your head?

ROCK COLLECTING

Rocks are so plentiful that in most places it is okay to pick some up and bring them home (but always ask permission first).

HERE'S WHAT YOU NEED

Pail or bag

Egg carton

Newspaper

HERE'S WHAT YOU DO

1 Take a walk with a grown-up and gather some rocks in a pail.

2 Rinse off your rocks and spread them on newspaper. Are all of your rocks the same size, shape, and color? Pick out the one that is the most round. Now pick the largest, and then the most colorful. Can you pick out the one that feels the lightest? Are any of your rocks smooth?

3 If you want to save some for your collection, place them in your egg carton. Ask a grown-up to help you label the carton with the name of the place where you found them.

MORE NATURE FUN!

⭐ As you visit more places, you may find many different kinds of rocks to add to your collection.

⭐ See if your local museum has a rock collection and notice how the rocks are displayed.

⭐ Rocks make nice paperweights. If you find the perfect rock, paint a picture on it and give it to someone as a special gift.

TO MAKE A PAINTED ROCK PAPERWEIGHT:

WITH A PENCIL SKETCH A PICTURE ON A SMOOTH ROCK

PAINT THE PICTURE WITH ACRYLIC PAINT

TIE A RIBBON AROUND THE PAINTED PAPERWEIGHT AND GIVE AS A GIFT

Collecting Fun

Collecting things from nature like rocks — and other interesting things, too, like bookmarks — can be lots of fun. First you *find* them, and hold them, and look at them carefully. Then, you *sort* them into groups, or *categories*, that have something in common — like all the round rocks in one pile. Next, ask a grown-up to help you find a book about rocks with pictures. Now you can try to *identify*, or name, each kind of rock and learn more about it. Last, you might make a *display* for your collection so that you can share what you learned with others.

PEBBLE GAME

Pebbles are small stones. Are all pebbles alike, or are they different?

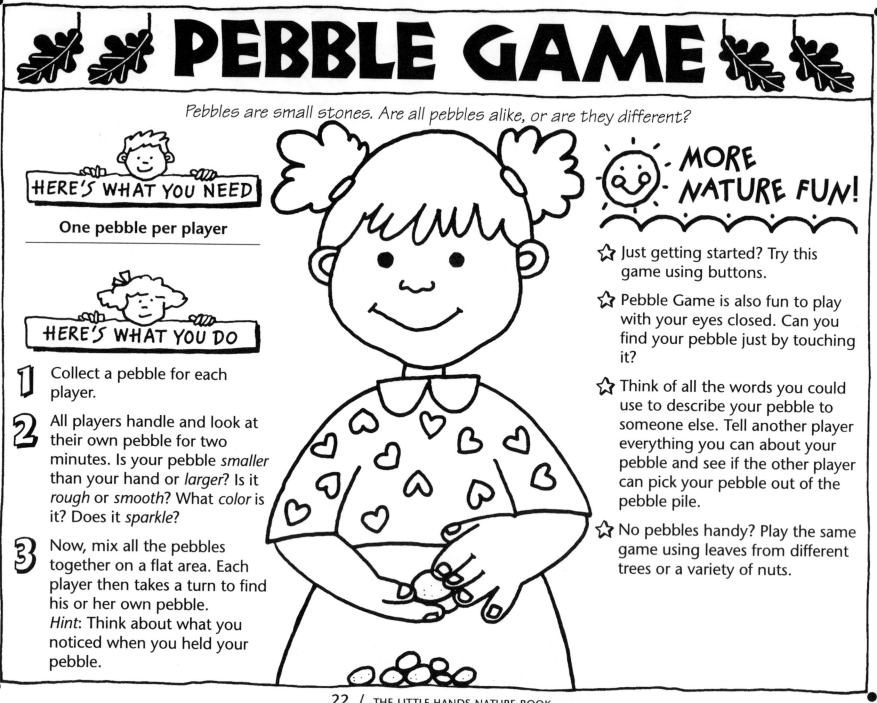

HERE'S WHAT YOU NEED

One pebble per player

HERE'S WHAT YOU DO

1. Collect a pebble for each player.

2. All players handle and look at their own pebble for two minutes. Is your pebble *smaller* than your hand or *larger*? Is it *rough* or *smooth*? What *color* is it? Does it *sparkle*?

3. Now, mix all the pebbles together on a flat area. Each player then takes a turn to find his or her own pebble.
Hint: Think about what you noticed when you held your pebble.

MORE NATURE FUN!

☆ Just getting started? Try this game using buttons.

☆ Pebble Game is also fun to play with your eyes closed. Can you find your pebble just by touching it?

☆ Think of all the words you could use to describe your pebble to someone else. Tell another player everything you can about your pebble and see if the other player can pick your pebble out of the pebble pile.

☆ No pebbles handy? Play the same game using leaves from different trees or a variety of nuts.

WEATHER WATCH

Sometimes from the bed I sneak,
And at the moon I do peek.
Oh, summertime is so much fun,
No time to sleep; where is that sun?

MAKE A WEATHER CALENDAR

There are no two days exactly alike. Each season brings different weather and each day new possibilities. Here's a way you can explore each season with your own weather calendar.

HERE'S WHAT YOU NEED

12 pieces of poster board
(8½" x 11" or 21 cm x 27.5 cm)

Markers and ruler

Outdoor thermometer

HERE'S WHAT YOU DO

1 Ask a grown-up to help you draw a monthly calendar on each sheet of poster board (7 boxes horizontally X 5 boxes vertically). Hang the calendar where you can write on it each day.

2 Hang the thermometer outside your window.

3 Each day at the same time take note of the weather. Draw a sun, cloud, or raindrops in the square for that day. Look at your thermometer and have a grown-up help you record the temperature for that day.

4 At the end of each month, count how many days it was sunny and how many days it rained. What was the *highest* temperature for each month?

MAY

72° 1	71° 2	80° 3	70° 4	72° 5	6	
7	68° 8	69° 9	75° 10	11	12	13
14	15	16	17	18	19	20

MORE NATURE FUN!

☆ What is your favorite kind of weather? Do you like the hot, hazy days of summer or do you like the brisk, cold days of winter?

☆ The temperature outdoors affects how people feel and what they like to eat. What would you bring to eat at the beach? What would you like to eat on a cold, Sunday afternoon?

☆ Here's a snack that is good any time of year. Spread a small square of date-nut bread with cream cheese. Top with another square of bread. Add in your favorite extras — banana, raisins, or honey.

Crash! Bang!

Here's a fun thing to do while you are indoors during the next thunderstorm. When you see a streak of lightning, begin counting seconds until you hear a thunder boom. Ask a grown-up to divide the seconds you counted by 5. If you counted to 10, the storm is 2 miles away (10 ÷ 5 = 2)!

SUNNY DAYS

The sun is a marvelous star, glowing 93 million miles away. We can feel the sun's warming rays when we step outside on a summer day. Here's a way that you can prove that the sun really does warm things.

HERE'S WHAT YOU NEED

2 shallow bowls

Water

Thermometer

HERE'S WHAT YOU DO

1 Fill each of the bowls with an inch or centimeter of cold water. Place one bowl outside in direct sunlight. Place the other bowl in the shade.

2 Check the temperature of the water in each bowl when you set them out.

3 Let the bowls sit for one hour. Then check the water temperature in each bowl again. Are they the same? Which bowl is warmer?

IMPATIENS
GROW IN SHADE

SUNFLOWERS
GROW IN THE SUN

MORE NATURE FUN!

☆ Try feeling the ground in the sunny spot. Now feel the shaded ground. Talk about the cool areas around your house and the warmer areas. Does *cool* equal *shaded* and *warm* equal *sunshine*? What does that tell you about the sun's rays?

☆ Some plants grow better in shaded places and others in sunny spots. Can you see different kinds of plants growing in each place? Do any plants grow in both sunny and shaded areas? If you were a plant, where would you like to be planted?

☆ Many flowering plants prefer sunny locations, but colorful impatiens likes the shade. Ask a grown-up to help you plant some impatiens in a shaded place outdoors or in a shaded window box.

WINDY DAYS

Wind is one of those things that you really can't see, but you can always tell when it is blowing! Here is your chance to explore wind!

HERE'S WHAT YOU NEED

Kite or windsock

Windy day and a still day

HERE'S WHAT YOU DO

1. Visit an area on a windy day. Can you see the wind? You may not be able to see the actual wind, but you can sure see the effects of the wind on flags, trees, your hair, and your kite.

2. Fly your kite or windsock. Does it fly into the air? What is causing the kite to fly?

3. Visit the area on a still day. Can you feel any wind? Does your kite fly? Talk about what you see.

4. Count 5 ways that you can tell if the wind is blowing just by looking outdoors. Can you list 5 ways you can tell the wind is blowing if you stand outdoors with your eyes closed?

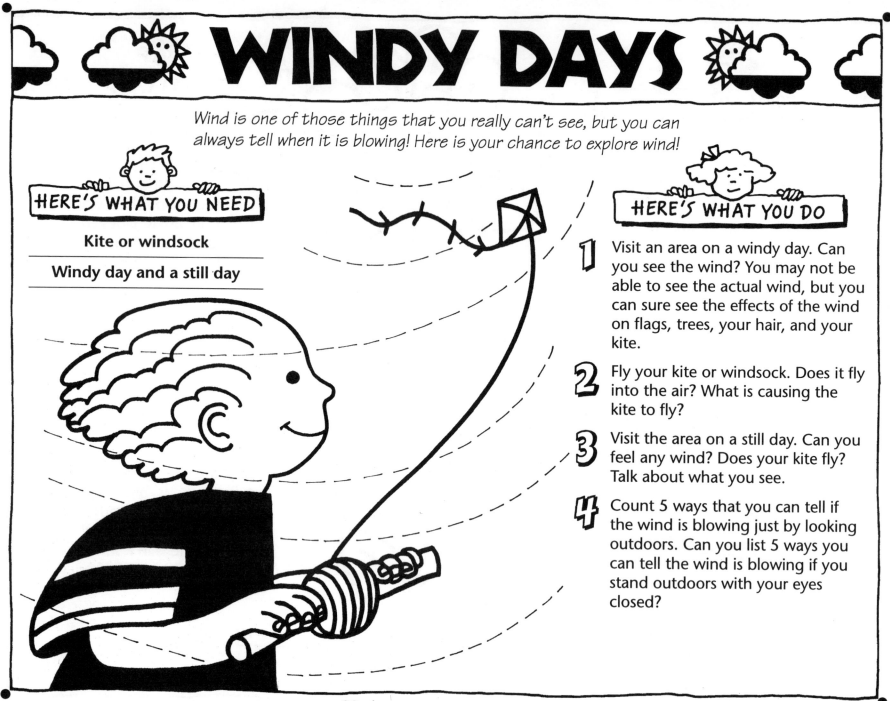

MORE NATURE FUN!

☆ Here's a great story to listen to on a windy day, *A Bed for the Wind* by Roger Goodman.

☆ Is there a barn with a weathervane or a windmill near your home? If so, watch it on windy days, and on still days, too. What's the difference?

☆ Join hands with some friends and run through a field on a windy day. Keep your arms spread out and let your hair blow freely. Can you describe what the wind feels like? If you could see it, what do you think the wind would look like?

☆ Pretend you are the wind. Now, pretend you are a tree blowing in the wind.

Blowing Winds

There are many different names for winds that blow throughout the world. A *williwaw* is the name of a cold, sudden wind that blows off the mountains of Alaska. In other parts of the world there are winds called *purga* and *sirocco*. We also describe winds with words like *breeze* or *gust*, depending on how hard they are blowing. Think about the other ways you can describe a wind.

AN INDOOR RAINBOW

Rainbows are so beautiful that some people think they are magical. You can make one outdoors (see page 43) or you can make one right inside your home!

HERE'S WHAT YOU NEED

Baking pan filled with about an inch (centimeter) or so of water

Small mirror

Sunny place inside your home

HERE'S WHAT YOU DO

1 Place the baking pan in the sunny place (on a table works best).

2 Dip the mirror into the water and hold it so that the sun hits it. Move the mirror until you are able to see a rainbow on your ceiling.

MORE NATURE FUN!

☆ Where else do you see rainbows? Look through a glass prism or a glass crystal. Make some home-made bubbles mixing ¼ cup (50 ml) liquid detergent and 1 cup (250 ml) water. Ask a grown-up to help you make a bubble wand with a wire hanger. Then blow rainbow bubbles in the sunlight.

☆ Read *The Rainbow Goblins* by Ul de Rico.

After the Rain

Rainbows can be seen often after it rains because the sunlight shines through the raindrops. Sunlight is made up of seven different colors — red, orange, yellow, green, blue, indigo, and violet. Those colors are always around you, but not easily seen. See how many of those colors you can see in your rainbow.

CURIOUS CLOUDS

Sometimes we get so busy on sunny days we don't take the time to watch the clouds float by. Here's your chance to watch a show that goes on above our heads almost every day.

HERE'S WHAT YOU NEED

Blanket

HERE'S WHAT YOU DO

1 Spread your blanket on the ground and lie on your back. Do you see *thin, wispy* clouds or *big, fluffy* clouds? Are they moving? How many different kinds of clouds can you see?

2 What do the fluffy clouds look like? Do they remind you of any animals? Pick out a cloud picture and see if your friends can point to the cloud you describe.

3 Look at clouds on different days. Do they look the same? What do the clouds look like before a rainstorm?

MORE NATURE FUN!

⭐ Listen to the weather forecast. What is the difference between *partly sunny* and *partly cloudy*? Make up your own weather report at the end of the day. Does it match the forecast?

⭐ Make a cloud picture using cotton balls on construction paper.

⭐ Read *Dreams* by Peter Spier.

⭐ Make your own tiny cloud each time your breath hits the cold winter air.

⭐ The next time you're out in the fog, just think of yourself in the midst of a cloud! What's it like in there?

CIRRUS CLOUDS ARE THE HIGHEST

CUMULUS CLOUDS FORM WHEN WARM AIR BUBBLES RISE AND COOL

NIMBOSTRATUS CLOUDS ARE FORMATIONS OF WATER DROPLETS AND FALL AS RAIN

WISE OWL

Sky High

Clouds that are different shapes have different names. The fluffy ones are called *cumulus* clouds. The thin, wispy clouds that look feathery are called *cirrus* clouds. *Nimbostratus* are true rain clouds. Which clouds did you see?

SIGNS OF WINTER, SIGNS OF SPRING

There are so many changes that go on between the seasons. How many can you see during the year?

HERE'S WHAT YOU DO

1 What season is it? What does the sky look like when you go to sleep? In the summer it gets dark later. In the spring you can see it getting lighter each night. As autumn comes it begins to get darker earlier.

2 What other changes do you see and feel? When is it warm enough to wear shorts? When do you have to take mittens and boots out of the closet?

3 What is the first flower you see in spring? What tree changes color first in autumn?

MORE NATURE FUN!

☆ Take a picture of the first flower that blooms in spring.

☆ Press the leaf that changes the earliest in autumn.

☆ Celebrate Groundhog Day. Recite "How much wood could a woodchuck chuck if a woodchuck could chuck wood" fast 5 times.

☆ Late in the summer, have an outdoor picnic and look for woolly bear caterpillars. If they are heavy with "wool," supposedly a cold winter is ahead.

WISE OWL

Hiding Out

According to tradition in the United States, February 2 is the day the groundhog, or woodchuck, comes out of hibernation. The legend is that if it sees its shadow, it returns to its burrow for another six weeks of winter. If it doesn't see its shadow, spring will arrive soon.

CROCUS

RAINY DAY SPRINKLES

Rainy days may be wet, but they can put sunshine in our hearts, too!
On a warm summer's day, rainy days can be the best time for exploring.

HERE'S WHAT YOU NEED

Rain gear (optional)

Finger-paint paper

Tempera paints

HERE'S WHAT YOU DO

1. During a light rain, without any thunder or lightning, dress appropriately and head outside.

2. What does the air *smell* like? How does it *feel*? *Taste*? Watch the rain fall on the grass, plants, and flowers. *Listen*.

3. After the rain stops, walk barefoot through a mud puddle. Do you notice different insects or birds out and about?

MORE NATURE FUN!

☆ Place a piece of finger-paint paper on the ground. Dab on a bit of paint. Watch as the raindrops create pretty pictures.

☆ Collect rainwater in a cup. Ask a grown-up to help you measure it with a ruler.

☆ Read *The Rainbabies* by Laura Krauss Melmed.

NATURE DETECTIVES

Keep your eyes and ears open
And look all around,
For the clues in these walks
Are sure to astound.

SPIDER SEARCH

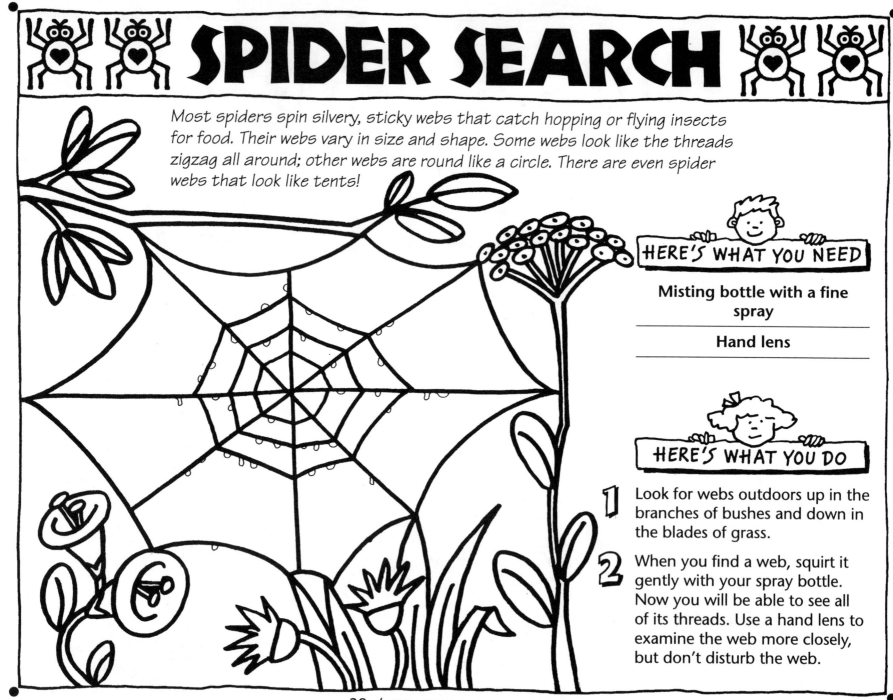

Most spiders spin silvery, sticky webs that catch hopping or flying insects for food. Their webs vary in size and shape. Some webs look like the threads zigzag all around; other webs are round like a circle. There are even spider webs that look like tents!

HERE'S WHAT YOU NEED

Misting bottle with a fine spray

Hand lens

HERE'S WHAT YOU DO

1 Look for webs outdoors up in the branches of bushes and down in the blades of grass.

2 When you find a web, squirt it gently with your spray bottle. Now you will be able to see all of its threads. Use a hand lens to examine the web more closely, but don't disturb the web.

MAKE YOUR OWN WEB

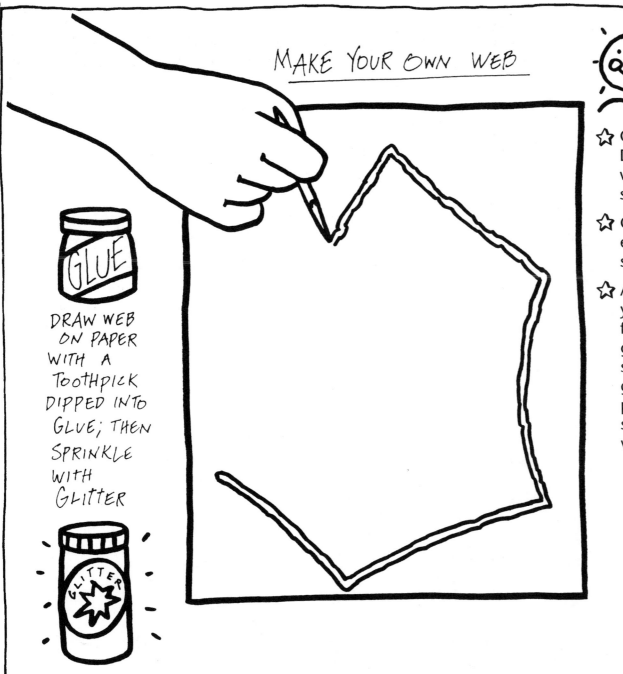

DRAW WEB ON PAPER WITH A TOOTHPICK DIPPED INTO GLUE; THEN SPRINKLE WITH GLITTER

GLUE

GLITTER

MORE NATURE FUN!

☆ Count how many spiders you see. Do they all look the same? Do the webs have different shapes and sizes?

☆ Count how many legs are on each spider. Do they all have the same number of legs?

☆ After your search, you can make your own web. You will need a few sheets of construction paper, glue, toothpicks, and glitter (or sand). Dip the toothpick into the glue and draw your web on the paper. Sprinkle glitter all over the sheet and shake off extra. Is your web zigzagged or round?

EENCY, WEENCY SPIDER

"The eency, weency spider climbed up the water spout,
Down came the rain and washed the spider out.
Out came the sun and dried up all the rain
And the eency, weency spider climbed up the spout again."

HERE'S WHAT YOU NEED

Paper towel tube

Egg carton section

8 black pipe cleaners

Glue

Yarn, triple the length of the tube

HERE'S WHAT YOU DO

1 Ask a grown-up to punch a hole in the top of the tube and thread the yarn through it.

2 Cut out one section of the egg carton and glue it to the yarn as shown.

3 Stick the pipe cleaners into the sides of the egg cup to form the legs of the spider. Double each pipe cleaner, so that the spider can stand.

4 Pull the yarn through the tube to make the spider go "up the water spout."

MORE NATURE FUN!

☆ Little Miss Muffet wasn't the only one to be surprised by a spider. Where is the strangest place a spider has ever surprised you?

☆ Ask a friend to read *Miss Spider's Tea Party* by David Kirk. Even though this story is pretend, or *fiction*, what do you learn about spiders that is true?

TO MAKE WATER SPOUT

PUNCH HOLE IN TOP OF TUBE — PUT YARN THROUGH THE HOLE

TO MAKE SPIDER

CUT AWAY ONE EGG CUP SECTION

GLUE YARN TO TOP OF EGG CUP

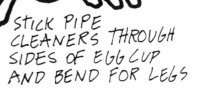

STICK PIPE CLEANERS THROUGH SIDES OF EGG CUP AND BEND FOR LEGS

PULL YARN TO MAKE SPIDER GO UP THE SPOUT

WISE OWL

Leggy Critters

If you counted eight legs on the spiders you saw outdoors, then you are absolutely right! Spiders have two main body sections and eight legs. Insects are different because they have six legs.

OVER-THE-RAINBOW HIKE

If you look carefully at a rainbow, you will see stripes of many different colors — red, orange, yellow, green, blue, indigo (a bright blue), and violet (a purple color). Keep your eyes open for pretty colors everywhere on this hike!

HERE'S WHAT YOU NEED

Crayons

Paper

HERE'S WHAT YOU DO

1 See how many of the colors of the rainbow you can find as you are hiking. Look for brightly colored flowers, green and autumn leaves, and colorful birds.

2 Use your crayons to draw a picture of one of the colorful things you see.

MY RAINBOW

MORE NATURE FUN!

☆ On a sunny summer's day, make a real rainbow with a garden sprinkler. Stand with your back to the sun and spray a fine mist in front of you. You can see the rainbow colors best in early morning or late afternoon.

☆ Read *The Mixed-Up Chameleon* by Eric Carle.

Colorful Creatures

Color is very important to animals and plants. It helps bees and butterflies find flowers to pollinate, it alerts some animals to danger, and it makes others attractive. Many animals, like chameleons, use their color for protection, by blending in with their surroundings. Sometimes the color becomes the name of the animal or plant, like a *blue* jay or an *orange*. What other plants or animals have a color in their names?

WHO WAS HERE?

We may not always be lucky enough to see an animal on our nature walks, but even if we don't, we might find the clues it left behind. What clues can you find on your walk? What animals do you think were there before you?

HERE'S WHAT YOU DO

1 Look for the following animal clues that might give you hints about the animal activities around you:

Snake skin

Galls: Look for bumps on leaves caused by insects.

Acorns: Look for insect holes and chew marks from squirrels.

Animal tracks: Look in mud and soft soil for animal footprints.

Eaten branches: How high are they off the ground?

Scat: Look for small round pellets left behind from rabbits, mice, or owls.

Deer run: Look for narrow trails of beaten-down grass.

Feathers

Bird nests

2 Play "Who Was Here?" Tell all the clues you noticed in one area, and see if you and your friends can guess who was there and what it was doing.

The Secret W's

When you are being a Nature Detective, use the Secret W's to help you figure out what has been happening around you:

Who?: Who do you think might have been there? An animal? A big bug? A bird?

What?: What might they have been doing there? Looking for food? Trying to escape? Making a nest?

Where?: Where did they come from and where were they going? Under a log? Up in a tree? Down a hole?

When?: When were they here? Last night? Early in the morning? A long time ago?

If you ask these Secret W questions, you might discover a lot that was happening that you never noticed before!

LET'S FIND GAME

Here's a fun way to sharpen your powers of observation, sort out what you see, and enjoy things you might have overlooked, too!

HERE'S WHAT YOU NEED

Hand lens (optional)

Binoculars (optional)

HERE'S WHAT YOU DO

1 Walk for a bit outside, then stop and look around you. See how many shapes you can find. Look for something *round*, something *square, heart-shaped, oval,* or *triangular.* After a few minutes start your walk again.

2 On your next stop see how many textures you can find. Look for something *smooth, rough, bumpy, slippery,* or *soft.*

3 Stop again when you've walked a bit further and try *counting* things you see. How many trees do you see? Boulders? Flowers?

MORE NATURE FUN!

☆ Describe the beginning sounds of the names of things you see. Say "buh" for bark, "kuh" for cloud, "chuh" for chipmunk.

☆ Now add a describing word that starts with the same sound, like brown bark, clear cloud, and chunky chipmunk. How many silly combinations can you make?

☆ Make tongue twisters with your silly sayings like, "The chunky chipmunk chattered while it chewed."

☆ Play "I See Something" indoors, outdoors, or in a car. Describe something you can see using shapes, colors, textures. ("I see something soft and brown. Can you guess it?")

FOLLOW-YOUR-NOSE HIKE

Have you ever taken a walk with a dog? Dogs spend almost all the time sniffing the ground, people, trees — everything and everywhere! Pretend you are an animal and see if you can follow your nose on this hike.

THYME   BASIL   DILL   MINT

HERE'S WHAT YOU NEED

Egg carton

A variety of strongly scented spices, including vanilla, cinnamon, cloves

Scissors

HERE'S WHAT YOU DO

1 Ask a grown-up to cut the egg carton into individual cups. Add a spice to each cup.

2 Have the grown-up place the spiced cups along a simple outdoor (or indoor) trail. Walk through the trail sniffing each scented cup. Talk about what each cup smells like. What does each smell remind you of?

MORE NATURE FUN!

☆ Walk the trail again to remove the spiced cups. Do you smell any other scents? Sniff the moist earth, blossoms, pine needles, marshlands. Talk about which scents are *strong, bitter, sweet, musty, pleasant,* and *sour*.

☆ How do you use your sense of smell? Can you tell what's for dinner just by walking in the kitchen? Can you tell if your Grandma has been visiting by the smell of her soap or powder? Now, imagine that you are a lost animal. How do you think a good sniffer will help you?

Smart Scents

The sense of smell is very important in the animal world. It is used to find food, locate other family members, sense danger, and to identify territories. Skunks have a different use for smell: When they become threatened, they release a strong odor to discourage anything from coming closer to hurt them. You do the same thing every time you put on bug spray to keep the mosquitoes from biting you!

ELF WALK

Some people say that elves and fairies live among the flowers. Do you think so? Try your hand at searching for some things these little people might use if they did live in the garden.

HERE'S WHAT YOU DO

1 Think about things found in the garden that a tiny fairy or elf would use for a bed, blanket, hat, dress, bowl, or table.

2 Take your imagination outside to see how many things you could use if you were a tiny elf. How about a soft-leaf blanket or an acorn-cap bowl?

MORE NATURE FUN!

☆ Listen to *A World of Flower Fairies* by Cicely Mary Barker.

☆ Ask someone to tell you the story of *Thumbelina*, or borrow the storybook from the library. Using a small jewelry box or shoe box, make a Thumbelina playhouse and furnish it with things from the garden and woods.

LOVE A TREE

To be a tree,
So wild and free,
There's nothing better
I like to see.

MEET A TREE

Have you ever been properly introduced to a tree? Here's your chance to personally get to know something very special.

HERE'S WHAT YOU NEED

Any tree

Hand lens (optional)

HERE'S WHAT YOU DO

1 Pick a tree to meet. Look at your tree from far enough away to see the whole tree. What shape is your tree? Talk about what it looks like.

2 Walk right up to your tree. Look at its bark. What does it feel like? Is it *bumpy* or *smooth*? What color is it?

3 Examine the leaves of your tree. What shape are they? Color? Fold one of the leaves in half lengthwise. Are the two sides the same?

4 Hug your tree. Can you get your arms around its trunk?

5 "Be" the tree. Spread your arms tall like the branches. Feel the sun, a squirrel in your branches, the wind blowing your leaves.

MORE NATURE FUN!

☆ Make a rubbing of your tree's bark by placing a piece of paper on the tree and rubbing a crayon firmly over the paper. Compare this rubbing to a rubbing from another tree. Are they the *same* or *different*?

☆ Adopt a tree: Take special care of your tree. Weed around its base; plant a few daffodil bulbs around its base in the fall; pick up any litter that gathers near it.

☆ Sit under your tree and read Shel Silverstein's *The Giving Tree*.

WISE OWL

Purposeful Parts

Each part of a tree helps to make it what it is. The leaves help make food; the bark helps to protect the tree from the weather, insects, and disease. The roots act like straws by drawing water and minerals up from the soil to the rest of the tree. They also anchor the tree in the ground. What do you think the branches are for?

MAKE-YOUR-OWN LEAF BOOK

Making your own leaf book is a great way to remember your leafing expeditions!

HERE'S WHAT YOU NEED

Blank book or loose-leaf notebook

Crayons

Clear contact paper and scissors

Nontoxic paint and paintbrush

PLACE LEAF ON BLANK PAGE OF NOTEPAPER; THEN PLACE CONTACT PAPER (STICKY SIDE DOWN) OVER LEAF

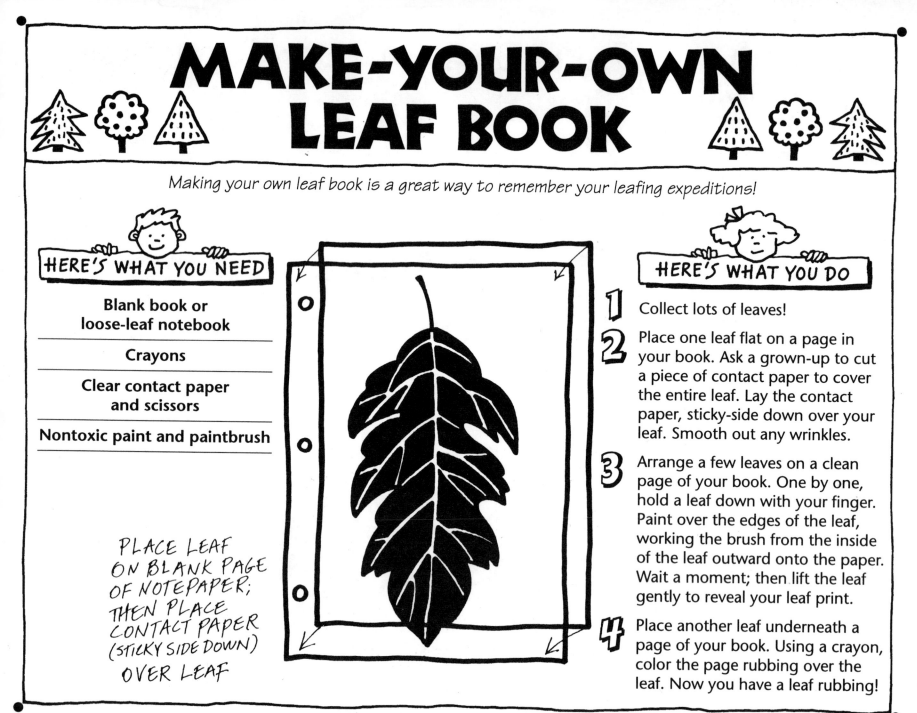

HERE'S WHAT YOU DO

1 Collect lots of leaves!

2 Place one leaf flat on a page in your book. Ask a grown-up to cut a piece of contact paper to cover the entire leaf. Lay the contact paper, sticky-side down over your leaf. Smooth out any wrinkles.

3 Arrange a few leaves on a clean page of your book. One by one, hold a leaf down with your finger. Paint over the edges of the leaf, working the brush from the inside of the leaf outward onto the paper. Wait a moment; then lift the leaf gently to reveal your leaf print.

4 Place another leaf underneath a page of your book. Using a crayon, color the page rubbing over the leaf. Now you have a leaf rubbing!

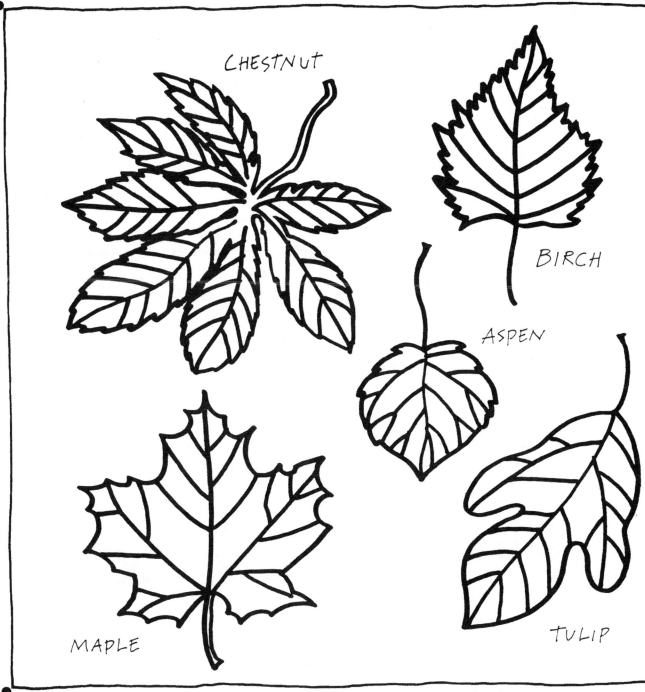

CHESTNUT

BIRCH

ASPEN

MAPLE

TULIP

Red and Gold

In the autumn months in much of the United States, throughout Canada, Europe, and northern Asia, many trees begin to lose their leaves. These trees are called *deciduous*, which means "falling off." Before the leaves fall, they turn bright red, gold, and orange.

Why do the leaves fall? In autumn, the weather is getting cooler, causing the trees to slow their growth. The water and sugar that flow through the trees also begin to slow down and eventually stop. There are fewer hours of sunlight that the trees need to produce their food. And last, a new layer of cells begins to grow where the leaf meets the twig, causing the leaf to finally separate from the twig.

PICK-YOUR-OWN

There are many farms throughout the country that will let you pick your own fruits and vegetables. In the spring you might be able to pick asparagus or peas. In summer, cherries and peaches are plentiful and in the fall, it's apple-picking time!

HERE'S WHAT YOU NEED

Sturdy shoes

Grocery bags or baskets

Insect repellent

Sun hat

Jug of water

HERE'S WHAT YOU DO

1 Ask a grown-up to call ahead to the farm to check on what fruits and vegetables are available for picking.

2 Plan your visit to the farm in the morning before it gets too hot, especially if you are picking summer berries.

3 Ask if the produce is sprayed with any pesticides before you sample your pickings fresh from the plant.

MORE NATURE FUN!

⭐ Apples, pears, peaches, nuts, and maple syrup are just some of the yummy foods that come from trees. Did you know that chewing gum and sarsaparilla are also made from trees?

⭐ Plan a buffet of tree foods. Can you make a whole meal from these foods?

⭐ Read *Once There Was a Tree* by Natalia Romanova. Then, tell about other critters that call a tree home.

PUT EVERYTHING IN A SAUCEPAN COVER, COOK UNTIL TENDER. COOL, MASH, AND EAT! YUMMY!

APPLESAUCE

WASH, CORE, AND PEEL 8 APPLES AND CUT INTO CHUNKS

1½ CUPS WATER

⅛ CUP SUGAR

1 TEASPOON CINNAMON

Homemade Applesauce

If it's apple-picking you enjoy, here's an easy recipe for applesauce to try.

Wash about 8 apples and ask a grown-up to peel and cut them into chunks. Place the chunks in a sauce-pan with 1½ cups (375 ml) water, ⅛ cup (25 ml) sugar (optional), and 1 teaspoon (5 ml) cinnamon. Cover the pan and sim-mer until tender. Let the apples cool slightly; then, mash them with a potato masher. Tastes great over ice cream!

PINECONE MOBILE

Pinecones can be found on trees called conifers that release their seeds by way of cones. The young cones are green and are closed tightly. As they get older they become dry and brown. Soon the cones open up and the seeds fall out!

HERE'S WHAT YOU NEED

Pinecones

A branch about 7" (18 cm)

Spool of cotton thread

Glue

Glitter

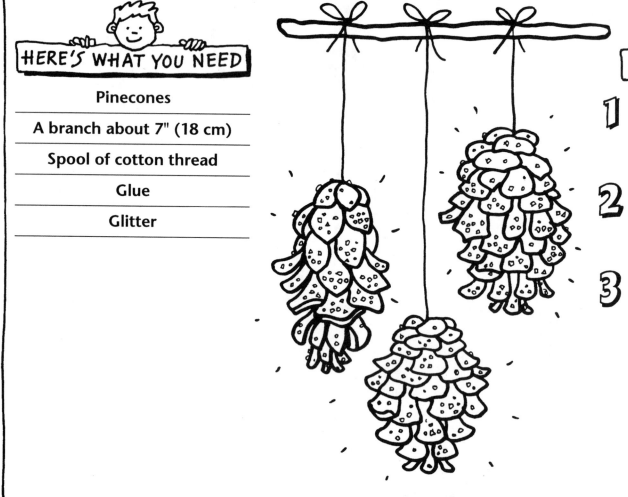

HERE'S WHAT YOU DO

1 Ask a grown-up to tie a piece of 18" (46 cm) string to both ends of the branch (for hanging your mobile).

2 Dab the glue onto the pinecones and sprinkle the glitter over the glue. Let the decorated pinecones dry.

3 Ask a grown-up to help you tie a length of string around each pinecone. Next, tie the strings onto the branch, letting the pinecones fall at different lengths. Hang your mobile in a sunny window and watch it sparkle!

MORE NATURE FUN!

⭐ Start a pinecone collection. Sort your pinecones by size into three groups: *small* cones, *medium* cones, *large* cones.

⭐ Make an elf house out of a small milk carton. Cover the carton with brown paper. Ask a grown-up to cut a door in the side that will swing open. Cover the "roof" with pinecone shingles!

⭐ What do you notice about trees that have pinecones? They have pine needles for leaves and they don't lose their leaves in winter.

MAKE AN ELF HOUSE

COVER A SMALL MILK CARTON WITH BROWN PAPER

DRAW A DOOR AND WINDOWS ON THE SIDES OF THE CARTON

ASK AN OLDER PERSON TO CUT 2 SIDES OF THE DOOR SO THAT IT WILL OPEN AND SHUT; THEN GLUE ON PINECONE ROOF SHINGLES

WISE OWL

Up to the Sky

What is the biggest living organism on the Earth? Is it the elephant or the whale? No. It is the *giant redwood tree* of California, a conifer that grows to 100 meters (325 feet) tall. That's as tall as a 13-story building!

Another conifer also sets records in the natural kingdom: The *bristle-cone pines* in the southwestern United States have actually been growing for 5,000 years — and still are!

LEAF MATCH GAME

Test your matching skills with this fun hiking game.

HERE'S WHAT YOU DO

1 Pick a leaf from a tree before you begin your hike.

2 Examine the leaf. Is it *pointy*? *Round*? *Smooth*? *Fuzzy*?

3 Begin your hike. Search for a tree that has the same type of leaf. How many trees can you find with the same leaf?

WISE OWL

Sort Them Out

Notice that the leaf lines, or veins, in some leaves are *side-by-side in straight lines*; in other leaves, the leaf lines, or veins, look like *branches*. All leaves have one or the other pattern: straight lines or branches. Sort your leaves into these two groups.

MORE NATURE FUN!

☆ Make a leaf person. Press your leaf in a phone book for a couple days. Then, glue it to a piece of construction paper. This will be your leaf person's body. Draw a head, arms, and legs with a crayon.

☆ Collect a big bunch of colorful autumn leaves. Arrange them in a glass for an autumn-leaf bouquet.

☆ Collect a bunch of green leaves. Trace each one on some paper. See all the different shapes! Look in a leaf identification book with a grown-up.

STARRY NIGHTS

When day is done
And the stars alight
And all the critters know it's night,
You'll be surprised at what you find
Flutters and flashes
Oh, what a sight!

FIREFLY PICNIC

A warm summer's evening is the perfect setting for a firefly picnic. Pack a delicious evening treat and spread your blanket out under the stars!

HERE'S WHAT YOU NEED

Flashlight

Wide-mouthed jar

Rubber band

Sheet of paper
to cover mouth of jar

Picnic blanket

Evening snack

HERE'S WHAT YOU DO

1 Plan to get started around dusk. Lay down your blanket and share your snack. Enjoy the cool evening air and watch the sunset if you can.

2 Make your own firefly lantern by following the twinkling lights to each insect.

3 Catch the fireflies with gently cupped hands and release them into the jar. Cover the jar opening with the paper and affix with the rubber band.

4 Poke some tiny holes in the cover and watch your lamp twinkle! When you are ready to leave for the night, remember to set your fireflies free.

MORE NATURE FUN!

☆ Make an evening snack of bread and jam with some "Bug Juice" to wash it down. Here's the recipe for Bug Juice: Mix three kinds of fruit juice together (like orange, lemonade, and cranberry juice). Float some sliced oranges on top. Pour from a chilled thermos.

☆ Listen to the story *The Very Lonely Firefly* by Eric Carle.

☆ Fireflies are easy to spot in the dark. Use all of your senses to identify other bugs by their special appearances, sounds they make, way they fly or creep.

CATCH FIREFLIES IN CUPPED HANDS

PUT FIREFLIES INTO A JAR. COVER WITH PAPER SECURED WITH A RUBBER BAND.

POKE TINY HOLES IN PAPER COVER WITH TOOTHPICK.

LET FIREFLIES OUT OF JAR BEFORE YOU GO HOME!

WISE OWL

Smart Talk

Why do fireflies glow? Believe it or not, this is how fireflies communicate with one another. Notice that some fireflies shine steadily while others flash every now and then; still others use a pulsing pattern of flashes, turning their light on and off. Notice also that some fly in a straight line, while others can be found zigzagging across the sky. Do you wonder what they are "saying" to one another? Maybe that special glow when you set them free is a friendly, " Nice to visit with you. Thank you for letting me fly away."

OWL PROWL

"Sometimes there's an owl and sometimes there isn't," says Jane Yolen in Owl Moon. *She is quite right, but whether you see an owl or not, "owling" is a wonderful way to spend a moonlit evening in the winter.*

HERE'S WHAT YOU NEED

Flashlight

Bird guide

Owl hooter (optional)

HERE'S WHAT YOU DO

1 Before you start out for an evening walk, scout the area during the day. Look for wooded areas with bordering fields. If you see whitewash on trees or owl pellets underneath, it is a sure sign that there are owls around.

2 When you set out in the evening, dress appropriately for the weather and wear sturdy walking shoes. Be in place shortly before dark. Use your owl hooter to attract the birds. Make your own calls as well! Search the trees with your flashlight and be still, quiet, and patient.

MORE NATURE FUN!

⭐ Read *Owl Babies* by Martin Waddell.

⭐ Be a nature detective. List all the "evidence" you find that an owl has been somewhere nearby. Did you hear any big wings flutter?

⭐ Make an owl sculpture out of clay. First look at a picture in a bird book. Notice how it looks like the owl has no neck. Where will the eyes go and the ears? Make feathers with a toothpick or pencil tip. Now find a small stick to perch your owl on and place on your bookcase.

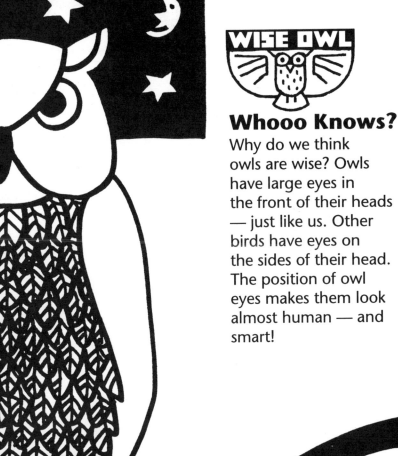

WISE OWL

Whooo Knows?
Why do we think owls are wise? Owls have large eyes in the front of their heads — just like us. Other birds have eyes on the sides of their head. The position of owl eyes makes them look almost human — and smart!

PICTURES IN THE SKY

You can have a star party on any clear night of the year.

HERE'S WHAT YOU NEED

Blanket

Star chart

Flashlight

Construction paper

Silver star stickers

HERE'S WHAT YOU DO

1 Ask your friends to bring blankets and place them where you all have a clear view of the sky.

2 Lie on your blanket and gaze up at the sky. Pick out a group of stars in the sky that make a picture.

3 Shine your flashlight on your paper and stick on the stars in the same pattern that you see them in the sky. Look for your picture in a star book. Does it have a name? If not, name it yourself.

MORE NATURE FUN!

☆ Make your own planetarium from a milk carton. Ask a grown-up to help you pierce holes in the bottom with a pin. Place a flashlight inside and aim the planetarium at a dark ceiling. Do you see starlike shapes on the ceiling?

☆ Look into the star-filled sky for shooting stars. These light trails are really meteors, or rocklike matter, falling earthward.

MAKE A PLANETARIUM

MAKE SEVERAL HOLES IN BOTTOM OF MILK CARTON

SLIP OPEN END OF CARTON OVER FLASHLIGHT, SET ON FLOOR AND SHINE ON CEILING

WISE OWL

Tell Me a Tale

Have you ever stared up at a star-filled sky and made a wish? If you have, you are not unlike all of the people who have lived before us and stared up at the sky at night. And people have always thought they saw shapes and objects in the sky. Long ago, they named these shapes, or *constellations*, and told stories about how they happened to appear in the sky. Take turns describing what shapes and pictures you see in the sky.

FLASHLIGHT HIKE

How is nighttime different from daytime? Find out by going on a flashlight hike.

HERE'S WHAT YOU NEED

Flashlight with a red bulb, if possible (red cellophane works well also!)

HERE'S WHAT YOU DO

1. Use a path that you are familiar with in daylight or stay around your own yard. You don't need to go very far. Keep as quiet as you can and stop often to explore.

2. Feel the ground. What does it feel like? Is it different than during the day?

3. Smell the damp earth. Place your flashlight at eye level and shine your light. Look for the eye shine of spiders and other critters.

4. Use your red flashlight to watch animals at night. They won't notice you if you are still and quiet. What do you see and hear?

MORE NATURE FUN!

☆ Talk about the *differences* between day and night.

☆ Listen to *Night in the Country* by Cynthia Rylant and *Stellaluna* by Janell Cannon.

☆ Why do you think some animals are *nocturnal*, or night, animals? Would you rather be a daytime or a nighttime animal?

☆ Using a stick, poke around moist areas with decaying leaves. Look for earthworms pulling the leaves into their burrows to eat.

Welcome!

You might be lucky enough to see some bats fly by early in the evening. Watch them as they swoop, and compare their flight to the way birds fly.

Bats are the only *mammals* that are able to fly. You and I are mammals, too. Bats are a welcome sight on a summer night because they eat 500 or more mosquitoes in an hour!

SUMMER SOUNDS

Summer evenings are filled with the sounds of insects, frogs, and other critters. See how many you can recognize in an evening.

HERE'S WHAT YOU NEED

Flashlight

Blanket or lawn chair

WHOOOooooooTY WHOOooo

CHIRRRRP CHIRRRRP

TWAANG TWAANG

BUZZZZ

BUZZZZZ

HERE'S WHAT YOU DO

1 Begin your evening exploration just after dusk. Be very quiet and listen closely. How many different sounds do you hear?

2 Listen for the *chirping* of crickets, the banjo-like *twang* of green frogs, the duck-like *quack* of wood frogs, the heavy *buzz* of June bugs, and the long *trill* of American toads.

3 Pick one sound and try to imitate it. Does the critter answer you? Can you guess where the sounds are coming from?

MORE NATURE FUN!

☆ Listen to summer sounds throughout the season. Do the sounds you hear change? Are they louder on hot nights than on cool nights?

☆ Make your own nature recording using a tape recorder to tape the sounds you hear. Then record some day sounds and some water sounds.

☆ Read *The Quiet Cricket* by Eric Carle.

WISE OWL

Nature's Jam Session

Crickets produce the chirping sounds you hear at night by rubbing their two wings together. Their chirping is the way they talk and call to each other. Unfortunately, their song also attracts bats and other critters who find crickets to be a delicious dinner. To prevent becoming dinner, the crickets all sing together in such a way as to "jam the frequencies" used by hunting bats. Some people love to listen to chirping crickets on a hot summer's night. It's music to their ears!

MOONLIGHT MOTHS

Have you ever seen moths fluttering around a light on a summer evening? Here's a way you can attract a lot of moths without a light.

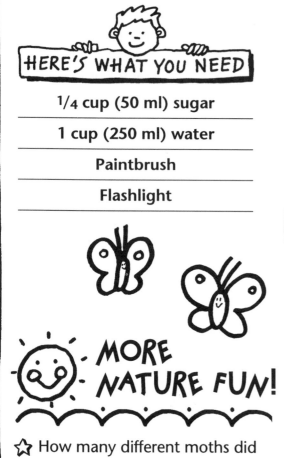

HERE'S WHAT YOU NEED

1/4 cup (50 ml) sugar

1 cup (250 ml) water

Paintbrush

Flashlight

MORE NATURE FUN!

☆ How many different moths did you see on the tree? Draw a picture of one of the moths. What colors do you have to use?

SUGAR WATER MIXTURE

HERE'S WHAT YOU DO

1 Ask a grown-up to heat the water and sugar together in a saucepan until the sugar is dissolved.

2 Paint a section of tree bark with the cooled sugar water just before dusk.

3 Visit the tree in the evening with your flashlight. What do you see when you shine the flashlight on the tree bark? Count the number of moths on the tree.

WISE OWL

Taking Turns

The nectar-feeding moths take over in the evening where the butterflies leave off during the day. Most of the moths spend their days resting in cool areas, awaiting their evening turn to feed.

SUN, SAND, AND SHELLS

Squish your toes in the sand,
Build a castle high,
Take a cool water dip,
Or watch a seagull fly.

SAND BETWEEN YOUR TOES

Sand is made by wind and water wearing away at rocks and shells until they become so small that they are called grains. A beach is made up of many grains of sand.

HERE'S WHAT YOU NEED

Sandy beach or a sand box

Sand bucket

HERE'S WHAT YOU DO

1 Ask if you can walk barefoot in the sand. What words would you use to describe how the sand feels on your toes? *Soft*? *Gritty*? *Hot*?

2 Find an area of dry sand. Scoop up a handful and try to make a sandball. What happens? Now pour some water on that sand and try it again. Which is better for making a sand castle, the *wet* sand or the *dry* sand?

3 Next, fill a pail with dry sand and fill another pail with wet sand. Can you tell which pail is *heavier*? Can you explain *why*?

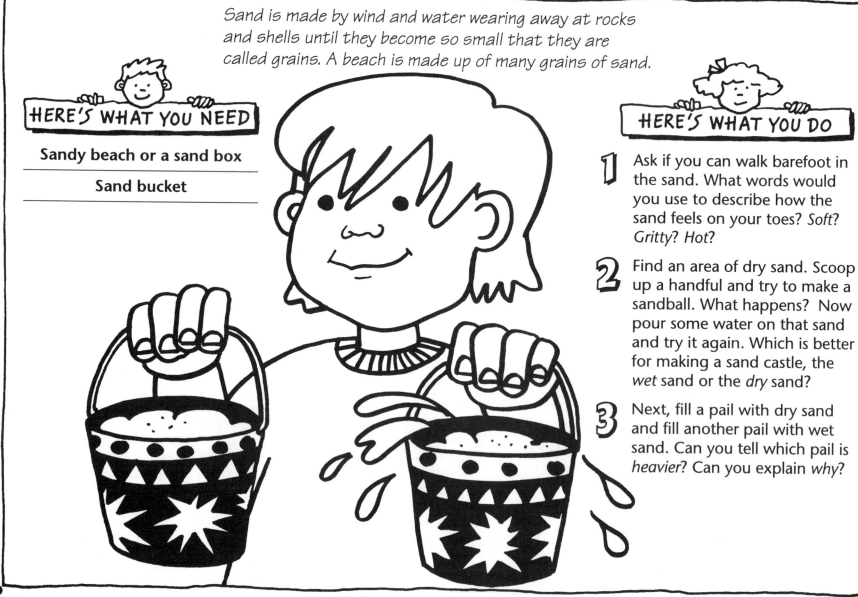

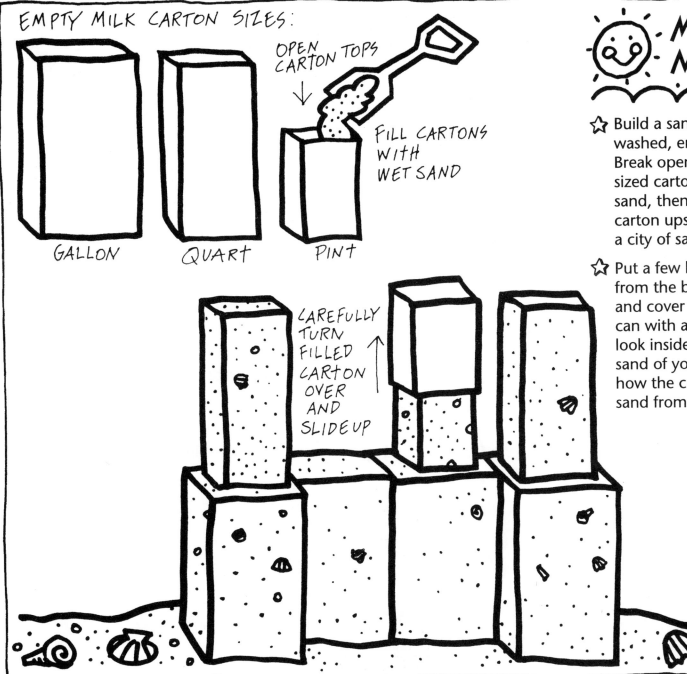

EMPTY MILK CARTON SIZES:

OPEN CARTON TOPS

FILL CARTONS WITH WET SAND

GALLON QUART PINT

CAREFULLY TURN FILLED CARTON OVER AND SLIDE UP

MORE NATURE FUN!

☆ Build a sand castle city using washed, empty milk cartons. Break open the tops of different-sized cartons, fill them with wet sand, then carefully turn each carton upside-down to create a city of sand.

☆ Put a few large pebbles or shells from the beach in a coffee can and cover with a lid. Shake the can with all your might; then, look inside. Did you create a little sand of your own? That's exactly how the crashing waves create sand from a rocky shore or coast.

BEACH WALK

As you begin to explore different beaches you will find that a beach at a lake is much different than a beach at an ocean. Some beaches have sand, while others are covered with rocks. You will also see the differences in shells, fish, and plants that wash ashore.

HERE'S WHAT YOU NEED

Sneakers or beach shoes

Hand lens

Pail and shovel

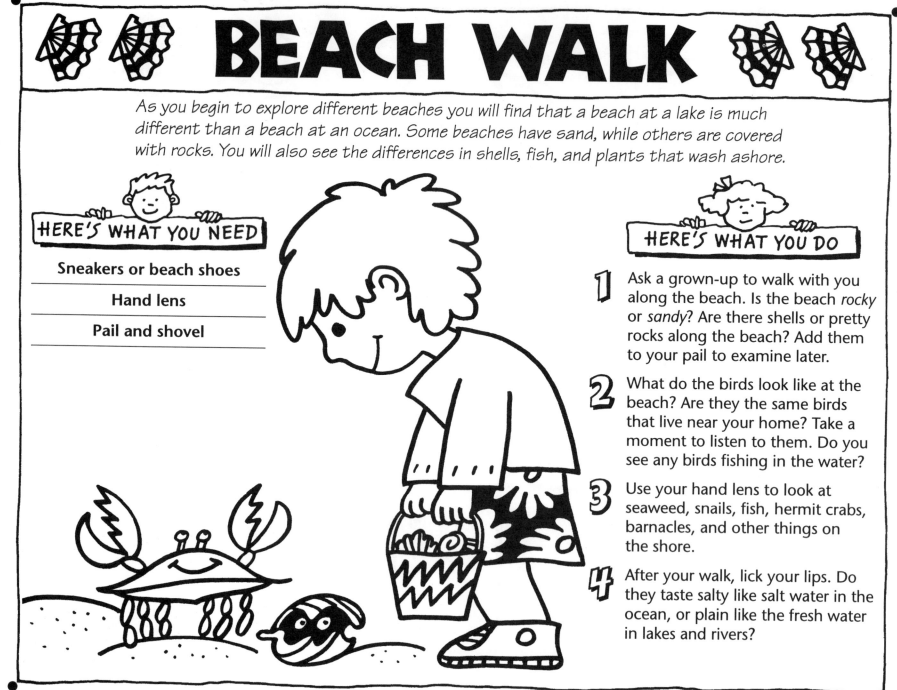

HERE'S WHAT YOU DO

1 Ask a grown-up to walk with you along the beach. Is the beach *rocky* or *sandy*? Are there shells or pretty rocks along the beach? Add them to your pail to examine later.

2 What do the birds look like at the beach? Are they the same birds that live near your home? Take a moment to listen to them. Do you see any birds fishing in the water?

3 Use your hand lens to look at seaweed, snails, fish, hermit crabs, barnacles, and other things on the shore.

4 After your walk, lick your lips. Do they taste salty like salt water in the ocean, or plain like the fresh water in lakes and rivers?

MORE NATURE FUN!

☆ Visit an ocean beach at low tide and high tide. At which time do you find more things along the shore?

☆ Read *Sea Story* by Jill Barklem (part of the Brambly Hedge series). Then, then have your own seaside picnic.

☆ Visit the beach with a grown-up early in the morning. Bring along a thermos of cocoa and sit quietly, listening to the beach sounds. What do you hear?

Scurrying Critters

As you lie on the beach listening to the water, you may not realize how many critters call the beach their home. Underneath the sand are shellfish and worms. Crabs scurry across the sand at the ocean hoping that they don't become lunch for hungry seagulls or sandpipers. And in the rolling waves at the lake are tiny minnows and sunfish eating tiny bits of plants. Ocean waves bring in jellyfish, starfish, and other wonderful creatures. Draw a picture of everything you see at the beach, but please, don't bring any living creatures home with you.

SEASHELL SEARCH

Shells are found at ocean beaches. You can also find shells of fresh water mussels and snails at inland lakes. So get on your shelling shoes to search for some of nature's most beautiful creations!

HERE'S WHAT YOU NEED

Shelling shoes or sandals

Pail

Net

Shell field guide

HERE'S WHAT YOU DO

1 Look along the beach for shells that have been washed ashore.

2 Walk along the water's edge with net in hand to catch shells that are caught in the waves.

3 Examine your findings on the beach and return any living creatures to the water. Talk about what lives inside each shell. Hold the shell to your ear. Do you hear the sound of the ocean?

MORE NATURE FUN!

☆ Start a shell collection. Wash your shells in soapy water. Dry them, and sort them by size, color, or kind of shell. Store them in egg cartons or empty containers.

☆ Make a shell wreath. Glue shells onto grapevine wreaths or a cardboard wreath shape. Add small pieces of dried driftwood, flowers, and sea grasses for a beautiful reminder of your beach visit.

☆ Make a pencil holder for your desk by gluing small shells very close together onto an empty frozen juice container.

☆ Glue some shells to a picture frame to hold your favorite beach picture.

Clamming Up

Many shells along the beach are the empty homes of *mollusks* such as clams, snails, mussels, and scallops. Clams bury themselves in the sand. They use a tube-shaped siphon to poke through the sand and suck water past their gills in order to breathe. If you find a clam shell along the beach, examine the shell's ridges. By counting these ridges you can tell how old the clam is.

EXPLORING TIDE POOLS

Tide pools, also called rock pools, are like miniature seas, complete with water and a community of wildlife.

HERE'S WHAT YOU NEED

Small net

Hand lens

HERE'S WHAT YOU DO

1. The best time to look for tide pools is when the tide has just gone out, and rock pools remain filled with water.

2. Sit quietly and look and listen carefully. Soon you will probably see some movement in the water. Look for anemones, crabs, small fish, starfish, and other creatures among the rocks. Do you see any hermit crabs?

3. Use your net to scoop out critters you would like to see a bit closer, but make sure you don't keep them out of the water too long. Use a water-filled pail to study them further, but then return them to the water.

MORE NATURE FUN!

☆ Visit an aquarium to see some other critters that live in tide pools. If you don't live near one, then visit a pet shop that sells fish. Ask to see the fish that live in ocean water and those that live in fresh water. Do you notice anything *different* about them? Anything the *same*?

☆ If you were a fish, would you rather live in saltwater or in fresh lake water?

☆ Draw an underwater mural with your friends. Place a big piece of brown butcher paper outdoors. Everyone gets some mural space, a paintbrush, and some paints.

WISE OWL

Star Light, Star Bright

The starfish is one star that doesn't shine, but it is special nonetheless. Starfish have arms called *rays* that are arranged in a star pattern. When a starfish loses an arm, it is lucky enough to grow another.

If you look closely, you will see the tiny tube feet that help the starfish move along the ocean floor.

DROPLINE FISHING

Here's your chance to play Huck Finn!

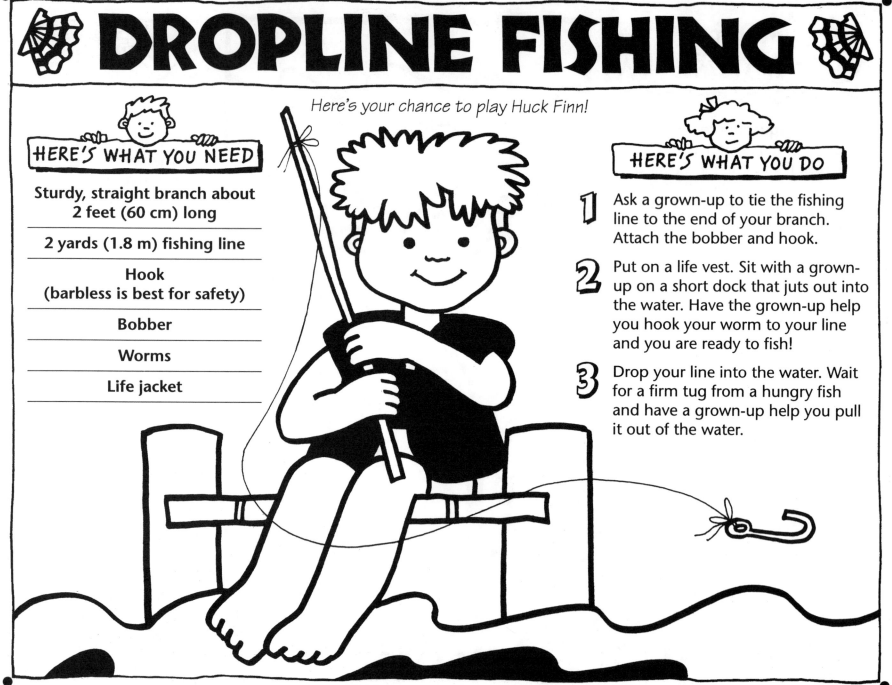

HERE'S WHAT YOU NEED

Sturdy, straight branch about 2 feet (60 cm) long

2 yards (1.8 m) fishing line

Hook
(barbless is best for safety)

Bobber

Worms

Life jacket

HERE'S WHAT YOU DO

1 Ask a grown-up to tie the fishing line to the end of your branch. Attach the bobber and hook.

2 Put on a life vest. Sit with a grown-up on a short dock that juts out into the water. Have the grown-up help you hook your worm to your line and you are ready to fish!

3 Drop your line into the water. Wait for a firm tug from a hungry fish and have a grown-up help you pull it out of the water.

MORE NATURE FUN!

☆ While you are waiting for the fish to bite, see how many kinds of fish you can name.

☆ Before you throw the fish back into the water, carefully feel the slippery scales on the fish's body. Don't touch the sharp fins, though. Look at the gills moving in and out, and the fish eyes.

☆ Measure each fish before you throw it back.

☆ Bring along a field guide to help you identify your catch.

☆ Have someone take a picture of you with the fish so you can show your friends.

PERCH

BASS

SEA HORSE

FISH BOOK

WISE OWL

The Breath of Life

All animals need *oxygen* to live. People breath in oxygen from the air; a fish can only get oxygen from the water. As the fish swims, it gulps water in through its mouth. The water flows over the fish's gills, which take out the oxygen. If the fish remained out of the water, it would not be able to live because it would be unable to take in oxygen. So what is the *same* about fish and people, and what is *different*?

SAND PICTURES

Sand has been used since ancient times to create pictures and to communicate.

HERE'S WHAT YOU NEED

Construction paper

Glue stick

Soft, fine sand

HERE'S WHAT YOU DO

1. Draw your picture on the construction paper with the glue stick.

2. Place the paper on some newspaper if you are indoors. Sprinkle the sand all over the paper.

3. Wait a moment and gently shake off the extra sand onto the newspaper. What fun — you've created an original sand picture!

MORE NATURE FUN!

☆ Start a sand collection from each beach you visit. Keep your sand in small baby food jars or film cases. Ask a grown-up to label each sample with the name of each beach. Is all sand the same color or is some *darker* and some *lighter*?

☆ *Texture* is how something feels. Is all sand the same *texture*? Is some *rougher* and some *smoother*?

☆ Divide some sand into several paper cups. Add a few drops of food coloring to each cup and stir. Now make your sand picture with colored sand.

CRITTERS

Every creature —
no matter how small,
no matter how loud,
no matter how insignificant it seems
— has a purpose on our Earth.

IF I WERE AN ANIMAL

If you were an animal, which animal would you be? Play this game on your next picnic and see what you can imagine!

HERE'S WHAT YOU DO

1 Make yourself comfortable. Close your eyes. Do you feel a breeze? Is the sun shining down on you? What do you hear?

2 Imagine that you are an animal sitting in this spot. Do you have thick fur, bright feathers, or scaly skin? Is the breeze blowing your tail? How do you feel, Pretend Animal?

3 Now, you are a thirsty animal. Where would you drink? Are you a large animal that would look for a stream or lake? Or are you tiny and able to drink from a puddle or the morning dew?

4 Pretend Animal, where would you live? Are there bushes nearby to hide in? Trees to scamper up? Perhaps some tall grass to slither in?

5 Open your eyes now. Talk about your Pretend Animal.

MORE NATURE FUN!

☆ Draw a picture and make up a story about your animal.

☆ Is your animal *imaginary*, or *real*, or *part pretend* and *part real*?

☆ Make a mask of your animal's face with a paper plate and some markers. Cut out weirdly shaped eye holes. Use some scrap paper or felt fabric to attach ears and a nose, and some feathers or yarn for fur. Stick your mask on a Popsicle stick. Now make animal noises that match your animal's size and shape.

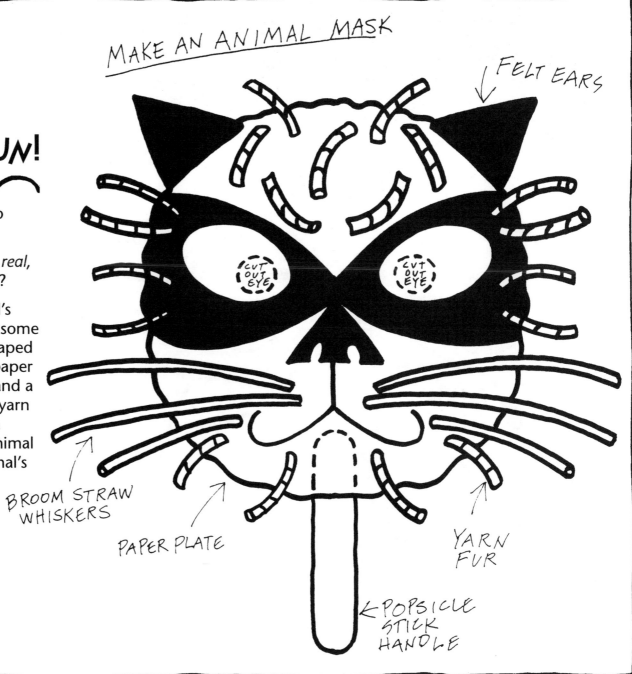

FELT EARS

CUT OUT EYE

BROOM STRAW WHISKERS

PAPER PLATE

YARN FUR

← POPSICLE STICK HANDLE

CRITTERS BENEATH

From tiny ants to large earthworms, let's see who lives under the rocks.

HERE'S WHAT YOU NEED

4 bricks or brick-sized rocks

Hand lens

HERE'S WHAT YOU DO

1 Place two of your rocks in a shady spot and the other two in a sunny spot. Visit your rocks each day. Turn them over very gently and look underneath. What do you see?

2 Each time, place the rocks gently back. Did you find the same critters under the rocks in the shady area and the sunny area? Which area had more critters?

MORE NATURE FUN!

☆ Count the critters that you see each day for a week.

☆ Ask a grown-up to help you make a chart for each area.

☆ Sit in the sun for ten minutes and in the shade for ten minutes. What are the differences? Which place do you prefer to play?

All in the Family

Did you know that an ant has a family? Ants, termites, and some bees and wasps live and work together in large family groups. That is why they are called *social insects*. Everyone has a particular responsibility like building or cleaning or searching for food. Do you have a special job in your family like setting the table or making your bed?

LEAF PEEPING

Among the green, leafy world of plants lives a whole bunch of tiny, wild creatures. Here's one resident you'll have fun getting to know!

HERE'S WHAT YOU NEED

Hand lens

HERE'S WHAT YOU DO

1 Look in the garden or bushes for leaves that have been chewed or torn, or where tiny brown droppings are found. Inspect around tomato, broccoli, or milkweed leaves (see page 101).

2 Look closely with your lens for caterpillars moving about or curled up among the leaves. Do you see their tiny legs? Can you see two oval eyes or a mouth chewing bits of a leaf?

3 Some caterpillars have a harmless fleshy "horn" to scare enemies that would eat them. Do you see any horns on your caterpillar?

MORE NATURE FUN!

Woolly Bears

☆ Critters have many ways of moving. Did the caterpillars you saw "inch" along quickly or crawl slowly? Can you think of times when you move *slowly*? *Quickly*?

☆ Watch the caterpillar for awhile. What do you see it do? Does it travel from leaf to leaf? Does it eat or remain still for a long time?

Have you ever seen a fuzzy brown and black striped caterpillar wandering the ground in fall? Then you've seen the woolly bear, the caterpillar of the Isabella Tiger Moth. Do you know any signs that signal the change of seasons? How do the animals act? How does the weather change? What happens to the trees?

ANIMAL TRACKS

Animal tracks, or footprints, help us to know what animals have passed by. Sometimes we can also tell what the animal was doing and where it was going, too. Here's a way that you can preserve an animal track to bring home.

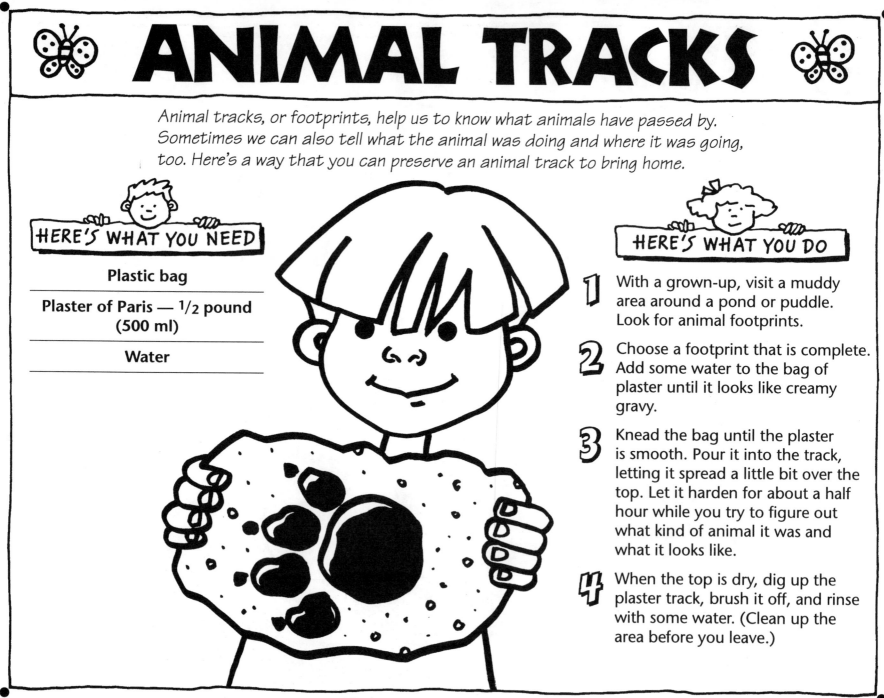

HERE'S WHAT YOU NEED

Plastic bag

Plaster of Paris — 1/2 pound (500 ml)

Water

HERE'S WHAT YOU DO

1 With a grown-up, visit a muddy area around a pond or puddle. Look for animal footprints.

2 Choose a footprint that is complete. Add some water to the bag of plaster until it looks like creamy gravy.

3 Knead the bag until the plaster is smooth. Pour it into the track, letting it spread a little bit over the top. Let it harden for about a half hour while you try to figure out what kind of animal it was and what it looks like.

4 When the top is dry, dig up the plaster track, brush it off, and rinse with some water. (Clean up the area before you leave.)

MORE NATURE FUN!

☆ Here are some other prints to look for: heart-shaped deer tracks, raccoon prints near streams and ponds, and opossum tracks in dirt and sand. Don't forget bird tracks in the sand!

☆ Tell a track story by drawing different-sized tracks on a piece of paper. Then ask a friend to "read" the story by explaining what was happening to the animals when the tracks were left. Were the animals playing together or was one hunting the other?

☆ Make a plaster cast of your own footprint or handprint.

ANIMAL TRACKS

DEER

OPOSSUM

RACCOON

ME

Fossils

Many fossils are no more than animal footprints that have been preserved for thousands of years. Visit a local rock shop or museum to see fossils. Then go fossil hunting, collecting rocks with interesting markings in them. Do you see any imprints that look like a fish skeleton or fern?

CREATE-A-CREATURE

Here's your chance to invent your own creature. Be sure to show how its size, shape, and characteristics affect how it moves, where it lives, and what it eats.

HERE'S WHAT YOU NEED

Old magazines

Safety scissors

Paste or glue

Scrap paper, 8¹/₂" x 11"
(22 cm x 28 cm)

HERE'S WHAT YOU DO

1 Find some interesting pictures of critters in a magazine.

2 Cut out the pictures and paste one on each piece of scrap paper.

3 Fold paper in thirds, and cut along fold lines right through the picture.

4 Now, mix and match the animals so you have the head from one, the body of another, and the feet of another.

5 Look at your creature and tell a story about it, showing a relationship between its body and how it lives.

MORE NATURE FUN!

☆ Get a book of animal pictures from the library. Have a friend describe an animal to you and then you draw it without looking in the book. Does your picture look the same or different from the book?

☆ Play "Who Am I?" by describing a real animal and having your friends guess what it is. Give plenty of clues.

Strange But True

A strange creature to learn about is the *duck-billed platypus* from Australia. It has a *bill* and *lays eggs* like a duck, but has *fur* like a mammal. Were the animals you created as strange as the platypus really is?

ANIMAL CHARADES

Here's your chance to act like an animal and not get into trouble!

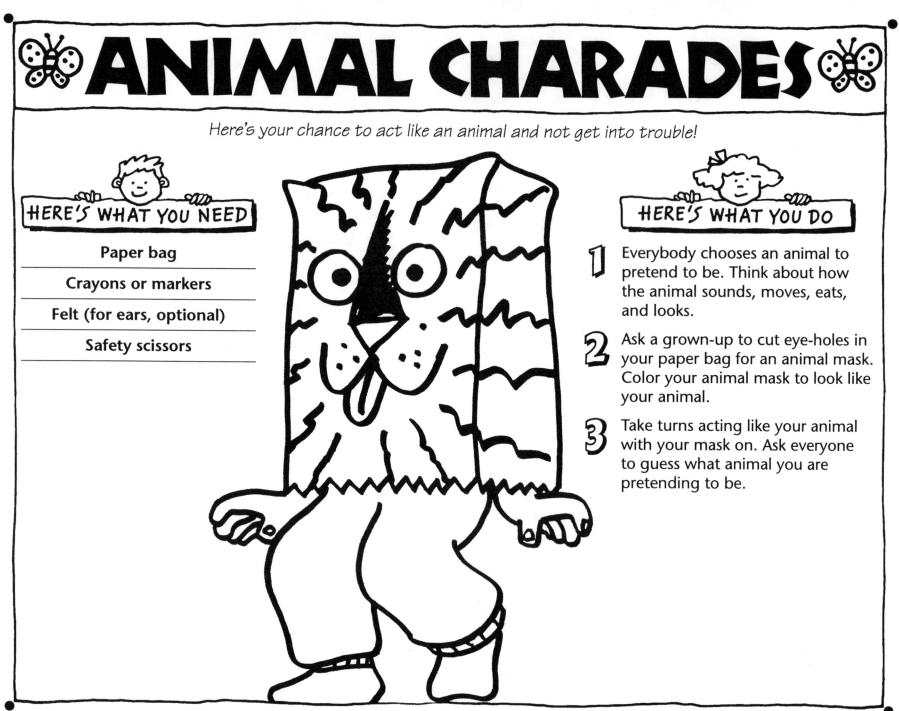

HERE'S WHAT YOU NEED

Paper bag

Crayons or markers

Felt (for ears, optional)

Safety scissors

HERE'S WHAT YOU DO

1. Everybody chooses an animal to pretend to be. Think about how the animal sounds, moves, eats, and looks.

2. Ask a grown-up to cut eye-holes in your paper bag for an animal mask. Color your animal mask to look like your animal.

3. Take turns acting like your animal with your mask on. Ask everyone to guess what animal you are pretending to be.

MORE NATURE FUN!

WISE OWL

- Do a finger painting of your animal. What details can you add that make your animal different from all other animals?

- What are your *favorite* things about your animal? Its big paws? The way it leaps or crawls? Its thick fur?

GIRAFFE

ALLIGATOR

They're Not Pets

All wildlife is just that — wild! That means you should never try to feed wild animals, or pet them, or pick them up, or take them home. Just look at them carefully from a safe distance. Try to memorize them in your mind so they will always be with you, even as they scamper away.

WORM FARM

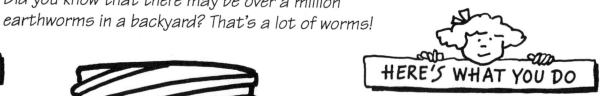

Did you know that there may be over a million earthworms in a backyard? That's a lot of worms!

HERE'S WHAT YOU NEED

Large mayonnaise-sized jar

Sand

Rich garden soil

Old leaves or compost

Water in spray bottle

Paper bag

Worms

HERE'S WHAT YOU DO

1 Place about two inches of sand on the bottom of your jar. Add about the same amount of rich soil on top of the sand. Continue layering sand and dark soil until the jar is 3/4 full.

2 Place the worms on the last layer of soil and cover them with the leaves or compost. Sprinkle the soil with the water to moisten the compost.

3 Place the paper bag over the jar to keep the soil in the dark. After a few days check your jar to see the tunnels made by your worms.

4 Keep the jar moist by sprinkling more water. Add more leaves and observe your worms again in 2–3 days. Make sure you set your worms free in your garden when you have finished your observations.

SEEDS TO GROW & SEEDS TO BLOW

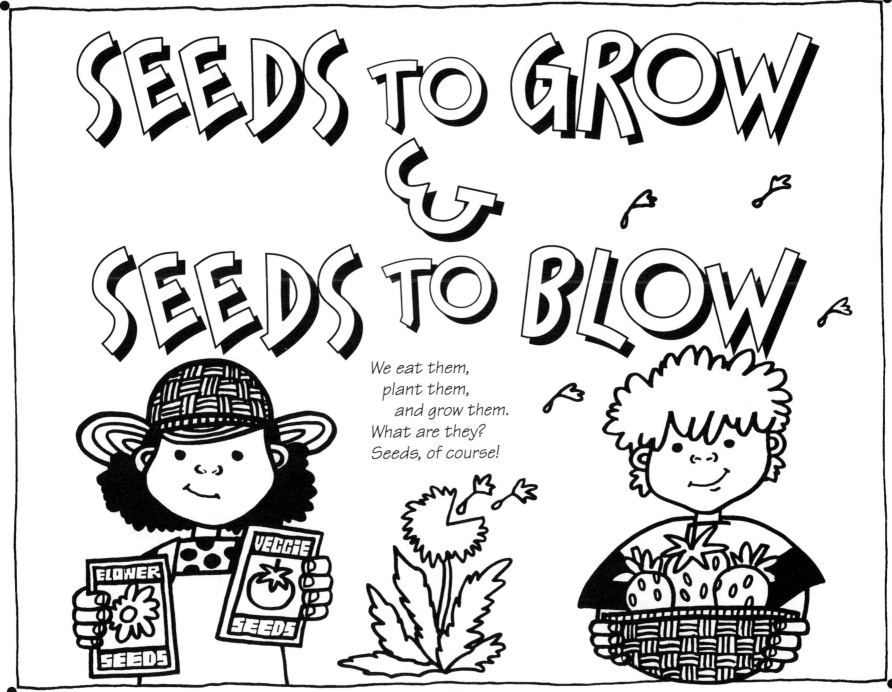

We eat them,
plant them,
and grow them.
What are they?
Seeds, of course!

FLOWER SEEDS

VEGGIE SEEDS

SEEDS FROM WEEDS

Milkweed seeds come in a little pod, attached to silky strands that blow easily in a breeze. Their silky tufts make soft pictures.

HERE'S WHAT YOU NEED

Milkweed pods (gone to seed)

Construction paper

Crayons

White glue or paste

HERE'S WHAT YOU DO

1 Search for some milkweeds. Look in a field for dried pods filled with white fluff.

2 Draw a picture or design. Milkweed fluff makes good hair, snow, clouds, and animal fur pictures.

3 Spread glue over the paper where you want the fluff.

4 Arrange fluff in glue. Finish your picture with crayons. Glue tiny seeds for other details or designs.

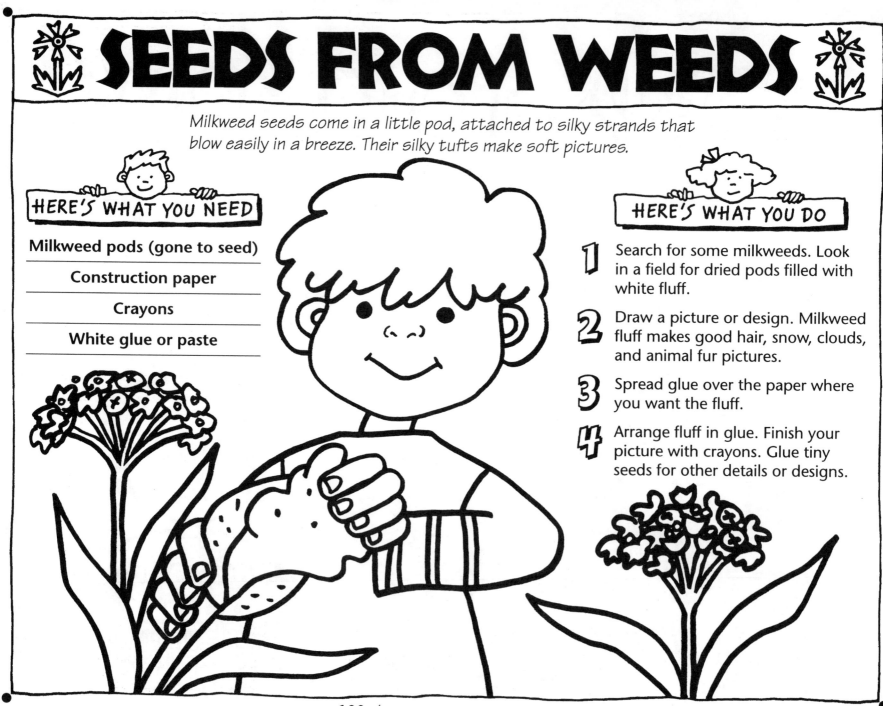

Leaves To Live On

The monarch caterpillar is a fussy eater, but it loves eating milkweed leaves. It can pack them in nearly as fast as we eat ice cream! Then it readies itself for an amazing change from caterpillar to butterfly. Look beneath the milkweed leaves for a hanging small, beautiful green pod, or *chrysalis*. Inside, the monarch grows until it emerges as a lovely butterfly.

TASTY SEEDS

There are many seeds that we enjoy eating. Some are so small, like strawberry seeds, we couldn't remove them even if we wanted to. Others are large and tasty all by themselves, like peanuts. Let's see which are the tastiest!

HERE'S WHAT YOU NEED

Strawberry

Raspberry

Sunflower seeds

Nuts

HERE'S WHAT YOU DO

1 Ask a grown-up to cut the raspberry in half. Do you see the tiny seeds *inside* the round parts of the berry? Do you taste the seeds when you eat a raspberry?

2 Can you find the seeds of the strawberry? Unlike other fruits, strawberry seeds are on the *outside* of the berry.

3 Taste the sunflower seeds and the nuts. Name other seeds you like to eat.

MORE NATURE FUN!

☆ Watermelon seeds are often in the way when you're eating. Next time you have watermelon, have a seed spitting contest. Of course, make sure you are outside! See who can spit the seeds the furthest; then, rinse off under the sprinkler.

☆ Some seeds, like in strawberries, are for eating; other seeds, like in apples, are not eaten. Make a list of fruit and vegetable seeds you eat and those you do not eat.

☆ Read *The Little Mouse, The Red Ripe Strawberry, and The Big Hungry Bear* by Don and Audrey Wood, or read Beatrix Potter's *Peter Rabbit*. Then, tell about other animals that might wander into the fields to eat the fruits and vegetables.

SEEDS TO EAT

STRAWBERRY
TOMATO
SUNFLOWER
PEANUT
OATS
ALFALFA
RICE
BLUEBERRY

SEEDS NOT to EAT

APPLE
PEACH
WATERMELON
AVOCADO
GRAPE
PLUM

WISE OWL

Great Grains

Some seeds that come from grasses are used for food. They are called grains. We eat them in cakes, cereal, and bread.

SEED SEARCH

Seeds are all around us — in our food, in our flower garden, and sometimes even on our cats and dogs! Let's see how many you can find!

HERE'S WHAT YOU NEED

Orange

Avocado

Grapes
(not seedless, of course!)

Paper and paste

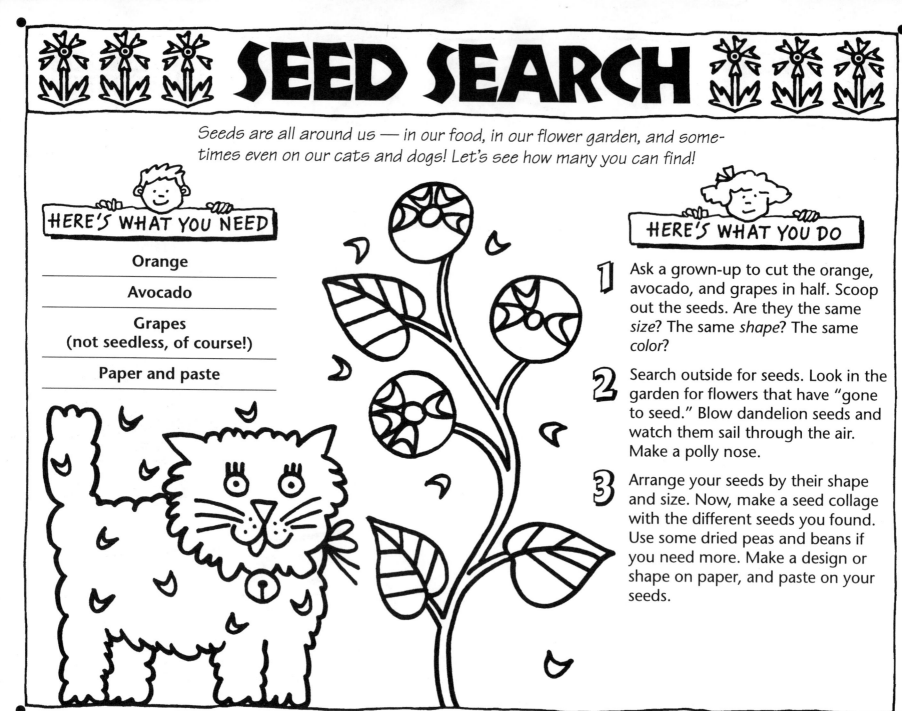

HERE'S WHAT YOU DO

1 Ask a grown-up to cut the orange, avocado, and grapes in half. Scoop out the seeds. Are they the same *size*? The same *shape*? The same *color*?

2 Search outside for seeds. Look in the garden for flowers that have "gone to seed." Blow dandelion seeds and watch them sail through the air. Make a polly nose.

3 Arrange your seeds by their shape and size. Now, make a seed collage with the different seeds you found. Use some dried peas and beans if you need more. Make a design or shape on paper, and paste on your seeds.

MORE NATURE FUN!

☆ **Start an orange plant:** Soak some orange seeds in water overnight. Line a pie tin with small pebbles. Add 1¹/₂" (3.5 cm) of potting soil. Press the seeds into the soil and moisten with water. Cover tin with a plastic bag and place in a warm, sunny spot. Watch for seedlings in about a week. Keep moist. You can transplant them into larger pots when they are at least 1" (2.5 cm) tall.

From Here to There

Seeds travel in some funny ways. *Dandelion seeds* float to the ground with tiny parachutes, *maple seeds* (those you can make polly noses from) whirl to the ground like helicopters, and *burrs* ride piggyback on animals and people. Now, pretend that you are a seed. Begin curled up, then reach for the sunlight and begin to grow. Blow in the wind or spin to the ground!

PLANT YOUR NAME

Picture your name in bloom! Here's a fun way to start your own personalized garden.

HERE'S WHAT YOU NEED

Seed packets of low-growing annuals, such as marigolds or nasturtiums

---

Shovel

Medium-sized stick or pencil

Small garden rake

HERE'S WHAT YOU DO

1 With a grown-up's help, clear a small area outdoors and loosen the soil.

2 With a stick, ask a grown-up to help you print your name or initials in the soil. Make it large enough to see when the plants begin to fill in.

3 Use your shovel to define the letters, by creating a small groove or furrow for planting your seeds.

4 Sow or place your seeds thinly in the grooves you have dug, and cover them over with finely raked soil. Water the seeds well, and water the seedlings whenever the soil looks dry. Before you know it you will have a personalized garden!

MORE NATURE FUN!

☆ *Name* all the colors you see in a flower garden.

☆ *Count* how many different kinds of flowers you see.

☆ *Smell* the different scents of the flowers.

Only Once

Annual flowers, like petunias, only last for one season or year, but they usually bloom for a long time in that season. You can cut them and more blossoms will grow back. *Perennial flowers*, like daisies, bloom each year, although usually for a shorter period of time. Visit a nursery to see annual and perennial flowers. Try writing a rhyme about a flower you see. It can be silly or serious.

HANGING SPONGE GARDEN

Here's how to have some fun with your leftover birdseed!

HERE'S WHAT YOU NEED

Natural sponge

Birdseed

Yarn needle and yarn

HERE'S WHAT YOU DO

1. Ask a grown-up to thread the needle with the yarn and make a loop through the sponge to hang it.

2. Soak the birdseed overnight in water. Then, sprinkle the seeds on the dampened sponge. Make sure the seeds go into the nooks and crannies of the sponge.

3. Hang the sponge in a closet until you begin to see sprouts; then move it to a sunny window. Continue to keep the sponge damp and you will soon have a fluffy hanging garden!

MAKE ALPHABET SPROUTS

DRAW AND CUT OUT A LETTER SHAPE ON 3 STACKED PAPER TOWELS

PUT SHAPES ON A PLATE, DAMPEN WITH WATER, AND SPRINKLE ON SEEDS

CHECK EVERY DAY TO SEE IF SEEDS HAVE SPROUTED

MORE NATURE FUN!

☆ Stack three paper towels. Draw a shape or letter on the top sheet and cut it out of each layer. Lay the stack on a dish and dampen the stack with water. Sprinkle seeds on the shape. Check the plate each day. It won't take long for your shape to sprout!

☆ Watch the sprouts reach for the light. Experiment with moving your plant. Does it always turn toward the light?

SEED MOSAIC

Seeds come in all sorts of shapes, sizes, and colors. You can mix them all together, or sort them out to make a pretty seed mosaic.

HERE'S WHAT YOU NEED

A piece of heavy cardboard

Construction paper

Craft glue

A variety of seeds

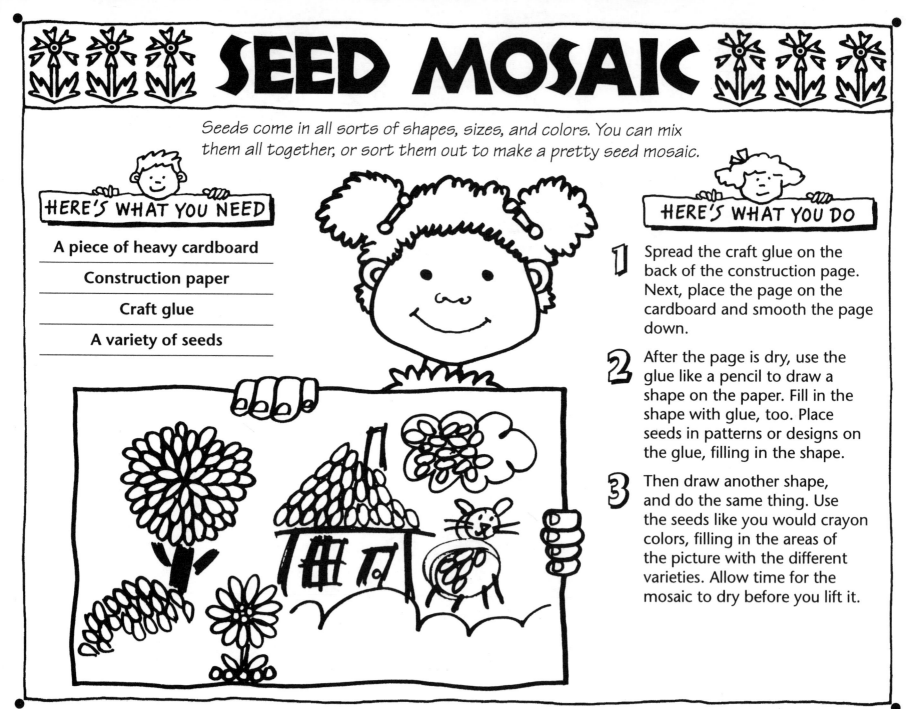

HERE'S WHAT YOU DO

1 Spread the craft glue on the back of the construction page. Next, place the page on the cardboard and smooth the page down.

2 After the page is dry, use the glue like a pencil to draw a shape on the paper. Fill in the shape with glue, too. Place seeds in patterns or designs on the glue, filling in the shape.

3 Then draw another shape, and do the same thing. Use the seeds like you would crayon colors, filling in the areas of the picture with the different varieties. Allow time for the mosaic to dry before you lift it.

FLOWER POWER

Roses are red,
Violets blue,
Be prepared here
To learn something new.

FLOWER POWER HIKE

With flowers, the more you look at them, the more you see.

HERE'S WHAT YOU NEED

Hand lens

HERE'S WHAT YOU DO

1 Choose a sunny, late spring or summer day to go on your hike with a grown-up. Look for blooming flowers in open fields, along quiet roadsides, public gardens, or in your backyard.

2 See how many flowers you can find of the same color. See how many of them have a smell, or *fragrance.*

3 Look at the *shape* of the petals on each flower. *Count* the number of petals each flower has.

MORE NATURE FUN!

☆ Plan your walk for early morning and see how many insects you find on dew-covered flowers.

☆ If you have permission, pick a couple flowers to press. (Lay flat between pages in your phone book.) Then, glue them to construction paper and hang on your door.

☆ Make candied violets: Pick flowers and leaves that have not been sprayed. Wash violets with their leaves. Use a small paintbrush to paint egg white on each flower or leaf. Sprinkle the painted flowers and leaves with sugar and lay on waxed paper to dry. Use the finished candied flowers and leaves as delicious decorations for ice cream, cupcakes, and other treats.

SPROUT SOME SUNSHINE!

Sunflowers begin as tiny seeds, but they can grow taller than you or me!

HERE'S WHAT YOU NEED

Sunflower seeds

Peat pots

Patch of garden

HERE'S WHAT YOU DO

1 Moisten your peat pot with water and watch it expand.

2 Poke a seed or two into the center of each pot and place in a sunny window.

3 Water your seeds each day. After they sprout, move them outside to your garden.

4 Dig a small hole for each pot in a sunny area of your garden. Allow for the growth of your plants. They'll get pretty tall!

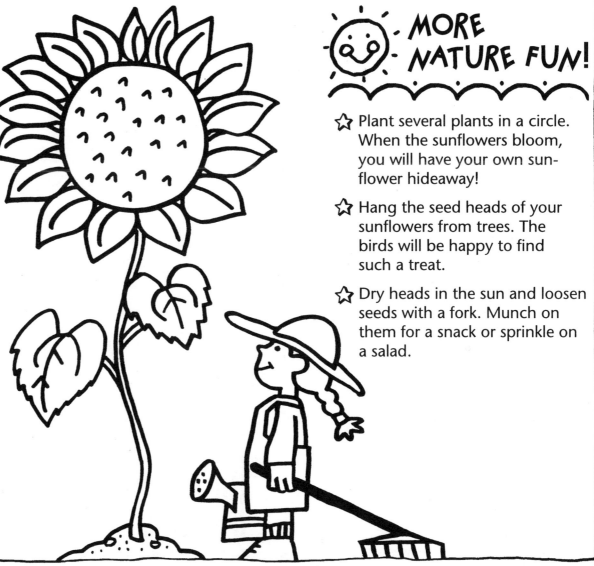

MORE NATURE FUN!

☆ Plant several plants in a circle. When the sunflowers bloom, you will have your own sunflower hideaway!

☆ Hang the seed heads of your sunflowers from trees. The birds will be happy to find such a treat.

☆ Dry heads in the sun and loosen seeds with a fork. Munch on them for a snack or sprinkle on a salad.

CREATE COLORED FLOWERS

If you wondered if the water you put in a vase really goes up the stem and into the flower, here is a way to see it actually happen!

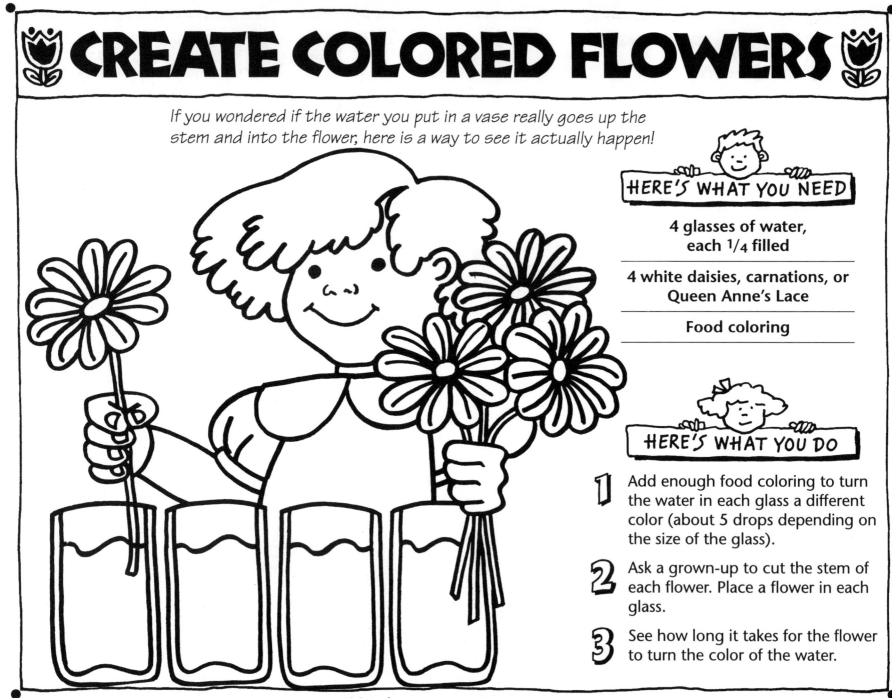

HERE'S WHAT YOU NEED

4 glasses of water, each 1/4 filled

4 white daisies, carnations, or Queen Anne's Lace

Food coloring

HERE'S WHAT YOU DO

1 Add enough food coloring to turn the water in each glass a different color (about 5 drops depending on the size of the glass).

2 Ask a grown-up to cut the stem of each flower. Place a flower in each glass.

3 See how long it takes for the flower to turn the color of the water.

MORE NATURE FUN!

☆ It is fun to have flowers around to experiment with and to do arts and crafts with. Go to a florist and ask if they have any flowers that have "gone by" that you can take home to play with.

☆ Take some flowers apart and look at them closely.

☆ Make a collage by pasting flower petals and leaves on paper.

☆ Hang some flowers upside down by their stems to dry.

☆ Put some petals in a bowl and leave them to dry.

☆ Make a book of pressed flowers.

Almost Magic

The stem acts like a straw drawing water up into the flower. As the colored water spreads throughout the flower it shows through the white, "turning" the flower another color. Make some colored flowers for a special holiday — such as green for St. Patrick's Day, red for Valentine's Day, and red, white, and blue for U.S. Independence Day.

FLOWER PRINT T-SHIRT

Practice on an old piece of fabric, before you try this on a T-shirt. These are so pretty that you may want to make one for a friend, too.

HERE'S WHAT YOU NEED

Flowers (daisies, pansies, and other "flat" flowers work well)

Leaves

Paintbrush

Fabric paint

HERE'S WHAT YOU DO

1 Ask a grown-up to wash and dry a T-shirt without using fabric softener. Place a piece of cardboard inside the shirt before you begin painting.

2 Hold each flower at the base of its stem and paint the top side with the fabric paint.

3 Lay the painted side down onto the T-shirt. Press lightly; then lift carefully. You should see the shape of the flower on the fabric.

4 Repeat the process using several flowers and leaves. You can add stems and centers to your painted flowers using the paintbrush or a cotton swab. Allow the shirt to dry overnight before wearing it.

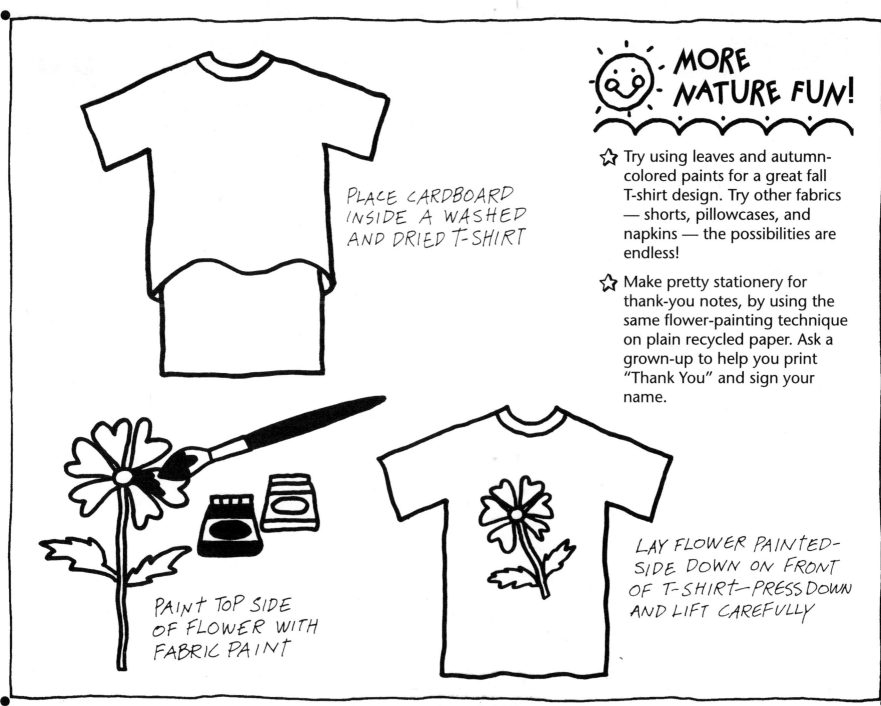

PLACE CARDBOARD INSIDE A WASHED AND DRIED T-SHIRT

MORE NATURE FUN!

☆ Try using leaves and autumn-colored paints for a great fall T-shirt design. Try other fabrics — shorts, pillowcases, and napkins — the possibilities are endless!

☆ Make pretty stationery for thank-you notes, by using the same flower-painting technique on plain recycled paper. Ask a grown-up to help you print "Thank You" and sign your name.

PAINT TOP SIDE OF FLOWER WITH FABRIC PAINT

LAY FLOWER PAINTED-SIDE DOWN ON FRONT OF T-SHIRT—PRESS DOWN AND LIFT CAREFULLY

FLOWER SUNCATCHERS

*When you hang something colorful in your window,
the light often bounces off it, brightening your room.*

HERE'S WHAT YOU NEED

Flowers

Heavy book

Contact paper

Safety scissors

Hole punch

Ribbon

HERE'S WHAT YOU DO

1 Press the flowers between pages of the phone book for at least 5 days.

2 Fold the contact paper in half and cut out a variety of shapes. You should end up with a pair of each shape.

3 Peel the paper off of one piece of the pair. Lay a flower on top of the sticky side of the contact paper shape. Cover with the other half — sticky-side down.

4 Ask a grown-up to help you punch a hole in the top of your suncatcher. Pull the ribbon through the hole and hang in a sunny window.

CUT OUT 2 CIRCLES FROM CONTACT PAPER

CUT OUT 2 TRIANGLES FROM CONTACT PAPER

CUT OUT 2 SQUARES FROM CONTACT PAPER

MORE NATURE FUN!

☆ Cut the contact paper into big shapes, such as a *circle* (trace around the bottom of a jar), a *triangle*, a *square*.

☆ Hang your suncatchers from a small branch to make a suncatcher mobile.

☆ Before you close up the contact paper, sprinkle tiny pieces of colored tissue paper or glitter around your flower for extra color power!

☆ Talk about the colors you see through your suncatcher. Are they the colors of the rainbow (see page 31)?

PLACE PRESSED FLOWER ON STICKY SIDE OF ONE SHAPE

COVER WITH MATCHING SHAPE STICKY-SIDE DOWN

PUNCH A HOLE IN TOP AND PULL A RIBBON THROUGH YOUR SUNCATCHER

COLORING WITH FLOWERS

Wouldn't it be fun to capture some bright flower color on paper? Well, you can — and draw a great picture, too.

HERE'S WHAT YOU NEED

White paper

Lots of different-colored flowers (buttercups, clover, marigolds)

Crayons or markers

HERE'S WHAT YOU DO

1 Hold a flower firmly in your hand. Rub the flower across the paper as you would a crayon. Did the flower leave any color on the paper?

2 After you have found which flowers leave color on the paper, you are ready to draw your own flower-colored picture. You can use the markers or crayons to fill in the colors that you need to complete your picture.

WISE OWL

Flower Talk

Of course, flowers can't talk but they sure can communicate. Their pretty colors and sweet smells appeal to lots of animals and insects — as well as you and me. A bright yellow flower "calls out" to a butterfly or bee, "Hey, see me? Come over here and visit me!" Even humming-birds are attracted to flowers by their scent and color (see page 130).

OUR FEATHERED FRIENDS

Some squawk, some chirp, and others tweet tweet,
Whatever their song, there's nothing as sweet.

HELP BUILD A BIRD NEST

Springtime is a wonderful time to see birds searching for bits of twigs, grass, and other things to build their nests. You can help them, too; then enjoy their nests and the sounds of young hatchlings chirping for food throughout the spring!

HERE'S WHAT YOU NEED

Brightly colored yarn

String

Cotton

HERE'S WHAT YOU DO

1 Gather together pieces of brightly colored yarn, string, and pieces of lint from the clothes dryer.

2 Place them outside on tree branches and shrubs where birds can snatch them for their nests.

3 In a few days look around the area for the bits of colored yarn and string peeking out of the nests the birds have made. If you look very carefully, you may see several nests made with your help! Please don't disturb them, of course.

 MORE NATURE FUN!

☆ Build a birdbath. Just like people, birds like to keep clean. Place a shallow bowl outside with some water for their very own bathtub!

☆ Name all the places you have seen birds. If you were a bird, where would you choose to live?

☆ Read *Cradles in the Trees, The Story of Bird Nests* by Patricia Brennan Demuth or *And So They Build* by Bert Kitchen.

 **WISE OWL**

Nesting

Most birds build nests to help keep the eggs and the baby birds warm and safe from enemies. Many birds, like robins and chickadees, build their nests in trees and bushes. Others, like the peregrine falcon, build their nests along rocky cliffs or, like swallows, in the eaves of barns and other buildings.

Sometimes baby birds fall out of their nests. If you find a baby bird on the ground, ask a grown-up to try to put it back in its nest. If you can't find the nest, place the bird in a nearby bush or tree. The parent bird will be looking for it.

FANTASTIC FEATHERS

Birds have three different kinds of feathers: down feathers, body feathers, and flight feathers. Feathers help birds fly and keep warm, too. You'll want to collect an assortment of feathers for this ticklish activity!

HERE'S WHAT YOU NEED

Feathers — flight feathers and down

Water and soap

HERE'S WHAT YOU DO

1. Collect and wash your feathers. Then, be sure to wash your hands with soap and warm water.

2. Allow the feathers to dry. Feel the difference between the smooth, stream-lined flight feathers and the fluffy, soft down feathers. Birds need their flight feathers to be smooth and straight in order to fly.

3. "Mess up" the flight feathers, then "zip" them back into place.

MORE NATURE FUN!

☆ Start a feather collection. Sort the feathers by *size* and *color*.

☆ Make a three-dimensional collage with the feathers you have collected.

☆ Make feather bookmarks: Place your feather on a strip of paper. Cover it with some clear contact paper, sticky-side facing down. Trim the contact paper. Now, find a bird book and mark your favorite page with your new feather bookmark.

COVER FEATHER ON PAPER WITH CLEAR CONTACT PAPER STICKY-SIDE DOWN; THEN TRIM

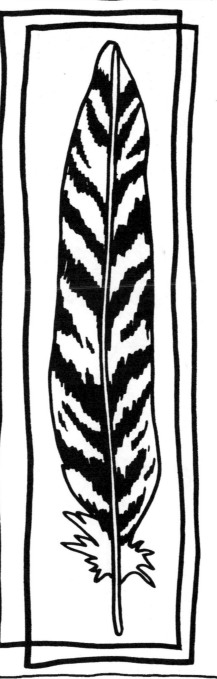

MAKE A FEATHER BOOKMARK

FIND A PRETTY FEATHER AND PLACE IT IN THE CENTER OF A COLORED STRIP OF PAPER

Looking Good!

Birds grow a new set of feathers every year. Watch as they "preen" themselves, or clean their feathers; then, they "rezip" them to get themselves ready for flight.

NOISY NESTS

Lucky for us, birds live nearly everywhere. They nest in trees, on cliffs, in marshy wetlands, too. We can't always see them, but we can recognize them by their cheery songs!

HERE'S WHAT YOU DO

1 Walk outside and sit on the ground. Do you hear birds singing? Listen quietly.

2 Keep your ears open for these special songs:

Chickadee — *chicka-dee-dee-dee-dee*

Barred Owl — *Who cooks for you? Who cooks for you all?*

Whippoorwill — *Whip-poor-will, whip-poor-will*

White-Throated Sparrow — *Ah, sweet Canada, Canada, Canada*

MORE NATURE FUN!

☆ Listen to the birds once or twice every month and write down what you hear. Do you hear some birds only in winter? In summer?

☆ Make up your own song about the birds; then sing it to them!

☆ While you are listening quietly, repeat the sounds you hear. Do the birds call back to you? Do they become quiet?

Heading South

When the weather turns colder and snow begins to fall, many birds go south, or *migrate*, to warmer climates. Then in spring, they make their return to enjoy summer where the temperatures are mild. Watch outside in fall for flocks of birds, such as Canadian geese, flying south. Do they fly in a special pattern? Are they noisy or quiet fliers?

HUMMINGBIRD FEEDER

Hummingbirds are so tiny that they often look like butterflies as they fly from flower to flower drinking flower nectar. They especially like the color red. Watch them at this feeder that you can make yourself!

HERE'S WHAT YOU NEED

Plastic soda bottle (1 quart or 928 ml)

Red artificial flowers

String

HERE'S WHAT YOU DO

1 Wash the soda bottle thoroughly and peel off the label.

2 Ask a grown-up to measure 1/4 of the way up from the bottom of the bottle. Pierce the bottle in the shape of an X. Make a square feeder hole from the X.

3 Remove the cap. Crease the bottle so that the hole remains under the crease in the front of the bottle.

4 Place a finger over the feeder hole and add the syrup. Replace cap. Decorate around the hole with the flowers.

5 Tie a string around the bottle's neck and hang from a branch. Refill your feeder every week.

Syrup Recipe
Ask a grown-up to help you prepare one part sugar to four parts boiling water. Cool completely.

PUT FINGER OVER FEEDER HOLE, POUR IN SYRUP, AND REPLACE CAP

REMOVE CAP AND CREASE BOTTLE HERE

Fast Flappers
Hummingbirds don't really hum. The sound you hear is the hummingbird's wings flapping so fast you may not be able to see them beating. They flap over 75 times per second and hummingbirds can fly 25 to 50 miles (40 to 80 km) per hour! How many times per second can you flap your arms? Per minute? Those hummingbirds really are speedy!

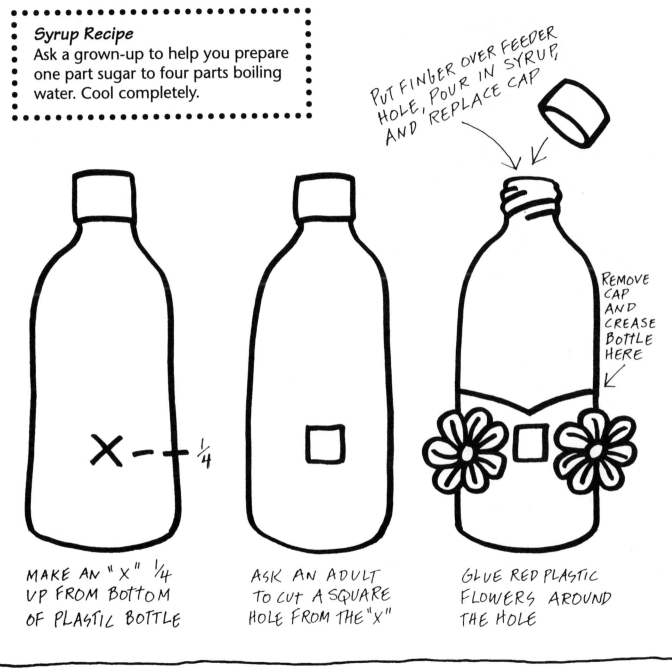

MAKE AN "X" 1/4 UP FROM BOTTOM OF PLASTIC BOTTLE

ASK AN ADULT TO CUT A SQUARE HOLE FROM THE "X"

GLUE RED PLASTIC FLOWERS AROUND THE HOLE

BIRD TREAT BASKET

Here's your chance to help feed the birds during the colder months. Watch and see which birds visit your feeders. Which ones eat alone, and which ones eat in groups? Which ones are messy, bold, or timid?

HERE'S WHAT YOU NEED

Scooped out grapefruit or orange halves

Birdseed, bread crumbs, raisins

Yarn

HERE'S WHAT YOU DO

1 Ask a grown-up to help you poke two holes in either side of each grapefruit or orange half. Put an end of the yarn through each hole and knot the end so that you have a basket effect.

2 Fill each basket with the birdseed and other treats.

3 Hang your baskets outside on a tree that you can see from a window. Watch to see who visits your basket. Remember to take down your basket when it is empty.

SNOWY DAYS

Days of sun and days of snow,
Here's more things you'll want to know.

SNOW PRINTS

If you look out your window the morning after a fresh snowfall, you might be lucky enough to see the tracks of animals that walked through your yard during the night. Here are some ways to explore snow prints before they disappear.

HERE'S WHAT YOU NEED

Boots and warm clothes

Tape measure

Field guide of animal tracks

HERE'S WHAT YOU DO

1 Ask a grown-up to help you measure the length of your snow boot before you go outside.

2 Find a clear patch of snow and walk 5 steps. Then run for 10 more steps. Look at your footprints. Are they the *same* or *different*? Ask a grown-up to help you measure one of the walking prints and then one of the running prints. Are they the same size as the boot you measured?

3 Find some animal snow prints. Ask a grown-up to help you measure the individual tracks. Talk about the animal that might have left the print. Was it a *furry* animal or a *feathered* friend? Can you tell if it was *running* or *walking*? Did it leave a tail print, too?

4 Look in your field guide to see if you can match the prints in the snow to the prints in the book.

MORE NATURE FUN!

☆ Follow the animal tracks and talk about what the animal might have been doing.

☆ Draw a picture of pretend animal prints in the snow. Then make up a story about the animal that left them. Are your prints *huge, tiny,* or *medium-sized*?

☆ If you live where it doesn't snow, where might you try these exact same activities outdoors?

☆ How would you describe snow to a friend who had never seen snow? Here are some words to start you off: cold, icy, crusty...

☆ Read *Snow* by Roy McKie and P.D. Eastman.

✳ SNOWFLAKE SNOOPING ✳

Take out your hand lens during the next snowfall and explore nature's marvelous artistic creations.

HERE'S WHAT YOU NEED

Dark piece of fabric or paper (allow to chill outside for a few minutes)

Hand lens

HERE'S WHAT YOU DO

1 Collect falling snow on the piece of dark fabric or paper.

2 Examine the snowflakes with your hand lens. Are they all the same? Look at all the different shapes. How many sides does each snowflake have?

3 Watch the snowflakes melt. How do their shapes change?

MORE NATURE FUN!

☆ Using white paint, glue, glitter, and cotton balls, create a snowy outdoor scene on a dark piece of construction paper. If you've never seen snow, ask someone to describe a snowy scene and then you draw it the way you think it would look.

☆ Draw as many different snowflakes as you can remember with glue. Sprinkle glitter or sand on the glue. Let dry and shake off excess.

☆ Make your own snowflake creations out of folded scrap paper. Ask a grown-up to show you how to fold and cut designs. Open up and hang in your window.

☆ Make sugar-on-snow. Bring a small bowl of clean, fresh snow into the kitchen. Ask a grown-up to drizzle some hot, pure maple syrup over the snow. Let it harden and then eat it!

MAKE YOUR OWN SNOWFLAKE

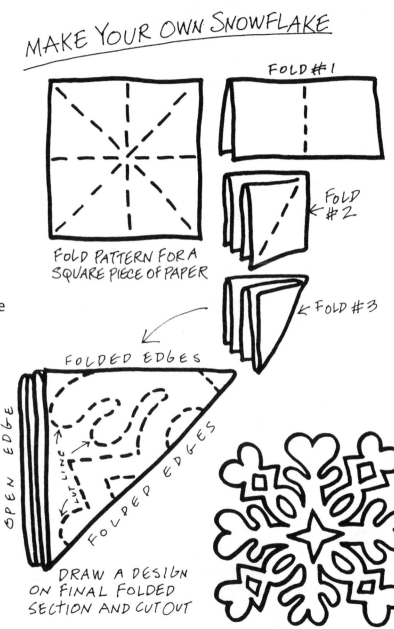

FOLD #1

FOLD PATTERN FOR A SQUARE PIECE OF PAPER

FOLD #2

FOLD #3

FOLDED EDGES

OPEN EDGE

CUT LINE

FOLDED EDGES

DRAW A DESIGN ON FINAL FOLDED SECTION AND CUT OUT

OPEN UP THE CUT OUT TO SEE YOUR BEAUTIFUL FLAKE

WISE OWL

No Two Alike

It's almost impossible to find two snowflakes that are exactly alike. This is because snow-flakes are created in a very special way. An ice crystal first forms in the sky, about two miles overhead, when a droplet of water freezes around a tiny particle such as a speck of dust. The new ice crystal changes shape as it falls toward earth; it usually bumps into other crystals, forming a one-of-a-kind snowflake.

WINTER WALK

The winter is a magical time to go exploring. Whether snowshoeing on a snowy path or hiking on a cold, clear winter day, you are bound to see things that you don't see in the warmer months.

HERE'S WHAT YOU NEED

Warm clothes

Sturdy shoes or boots

Binoculars (optional)

HERE'S WHAT YOU DO

1. Visit an area you are familiar with. As you begin your walk, look around your path. What is different in the winter than in summer?

2. Have a winter scavenger hunt. Look for things such as a bush with red berries, a pinecone, a bird, an icicle, a fir tree, animal tracks, and a squirrel. Look for something beautiful.

3. Sit for a short time on a stump or rock. How do you feel? What do you hear?

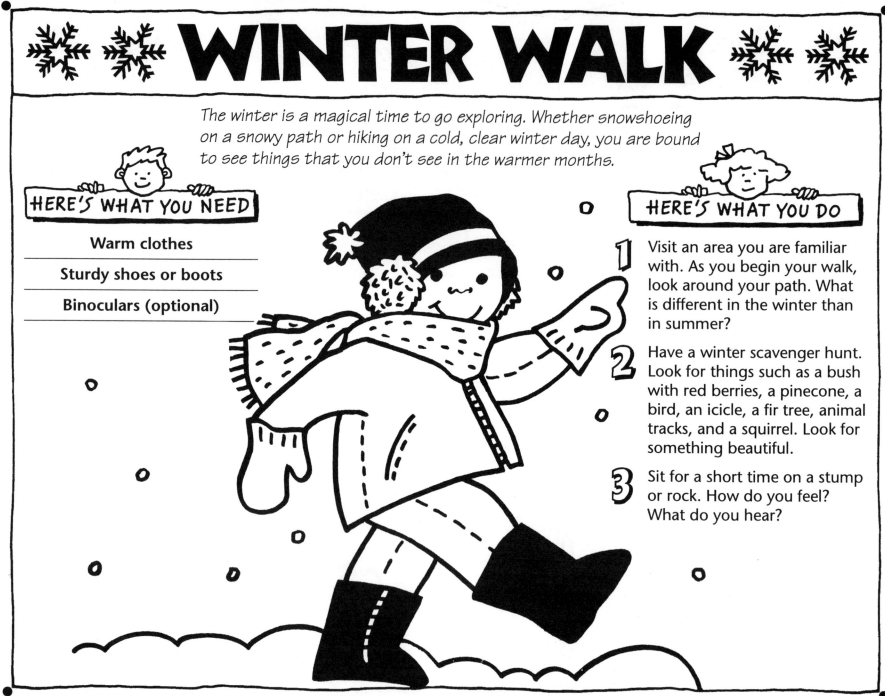

MORE NATURE FUN!

☆ Make angels in the snow or a snowman. Take out your sand toys and make a snow castle!

☆ When you get home, draw a picture of the woods in winter.

☆ Listen to "Stopping by Woods on a Snowy Evening" by Robert Frost.

☆ Ask a grown-up to help you write your own poem about the snowy woods.

☆ Watch the video *The Snowman* by Raymond Briggs.

WISE OWL

Ever Green

Evergreens are well prepared for the cold winter months. Unlike *deciduous* trees that lose their leaves in the autumn, evergreens, or *conifers*, have tiny leaves (needles), coated with wax that helps them retain their moisture. It's like putting lip balm on your lips to keep them from drying out in the cold winter wind. Evergreens also have sap running through their thick trunks, which acts like an "antifreeze," keeping the tree active during the winter. (See page 55 and 59.)

WHERE ARE THEY?

When the colder weather begins in the north, our wild friends get ready for the months ahead. Some birds fly south to warmer regions; some animals stay in the area but become less active — or even sleep away the winter! Even so, there are still many animals and birds that remain active throughout the winter. Here are some ways to look for them.

HERE'S WHAT YOU NEED

Binoculars (optional)

HERE'S WHAT YOU DO

1 Look for the birds that are wintering in your area at nearby feeders. Some to look for include beautiful red cardinals, noisy woodpeckers, and feisty little chickadees.

2 Look at the edge of wooded areas for nibbled branches and deer tracks. The best time to search is mid-day when many animals take advantage of the warmest part of the day to move about. Or search during a snowfall, or late in the afternoon, right before dusk.

3 Look for little piles of empty nut shells and stripped pinecones. These are signs of squirrel activity.

4 Use your *observation skills* to notice small hints that animals have been nearby. Do you see any prints? Any disturbed snow? Do you see any holes in trees or crevices in rocks where animals might live? The more carefully you look, the more you will see.

MORE NATURE FUN!

☆ Here are some hints for wildlife observation: Try to blend in with the surroundings. Hide behind trees, reeds, or boulders. Tuck a pine sachet or pinecone into your clothes the night before. Use a bird call. Keep the wind in your face so that the animal won't be able to smell you. Be still and quiet.

☆ If the animals don't *see* you, *hear* you, or *smell* you, they will just go about their business, and you'll get to observe them.

An Active World

There is a very active world lying just below the snow, too. Moles, shrews, and little field mice scurry along runways under the snow feeding on seeds and insects. Frogs are waiting out the winter beneath the ground and at the bottom of ponds. Deep beneath the ice on ponds and lakes fish swim around as they do throughout the year.

INDEX

C

caterpillars, 35, 90-91, 101
clouds, types of, 32-33
colors, 22, 31, 43, 84, 120
cooking, homemade applesauce, 57
counting, 25, 28, 39, 107, 112
crafts
   basket, bird treat, 130
   birdfeeder, hummingbird, 128-129
   collage, seed, 104
   creature, create a, 94-95
   elf house, make an, 59
   flower, 115
   mask, animal, 87
   milkweed seed art, 100
   mobile, pinecone, 58-59
   mosaic, seed, 110
   pencil holder, seashell, 79
   spider, make a crawling, 40-41
   suncatcher, flower, 118-119
   sundial, 18-19
   t-shirt, flower print, 116-117
   wreath, seashell, 79

D

drawing
   animal prints, 133
   with flowers, 120
   shadow pictures, 16-17
   snowy scene, 135
   story, animal track, 93

E

emotions, 17, 136

F

feelings, *see* emotions

G

games
   bingo, nature, 12-13
   charades, animal, 96
   imagination, 86-87
   leaf matching, 60
   observation, 46-47
   pebble, 22
   True or False?, 14-15

H

hikes
   beach, 76-77
   elf, 50
   flashlight, 68-69
   flower power, 112
   follow-your-nose, 48-49
   over-the-rainbow, 42-43
   owl observation, 64-65
   teeny, tiny, 8-9
   winter, 136
hummingbird feeder, 128-129

I

Insects
   caterpillars, 90-91, 101
   crickets, 71
   fireflies, 62-63
   hunting, 88-89
   moths, 72
   movement of, 9
   pill bug, 9
   social, 89
   sow bug, 9

L

leaves, 54-55

H

O

observation
   watch, 8-11, 34-36, 44-45, 52,53, 66-69, 72, 80, 88-91, 138-139
   listen, 86-69, 126-127
   game, 46-47
ocean, 80-81
owls, 64-65

P

painting, flower print t-shirt, 116-117
plants
   annuals, 107
   flowers, 111-120,
   garden, hanging sponge, 108
   perennials, 107
   sunflowers, growing, 113

LITTLE HANDS BOOKS FROM WILLIAMSON PUBLISHING

The following *Little Hands*® books for ages 2 to 6 are each 144 pages, fully illustrated, trade paper, 10 × 8, $12.95 US. Please see last page for ordering information. Thank you.

ALPHABET ART
With A to Z Animal Art & Fingerplays
by Judy Press

MATH PLAY!
80 Ways to Count & Learn
by Diane McGowan and Mark Schrooten

American Bookseller Pick of the Lists
RAINY DAY PLAY!
Explore, Create, Discover, Pretend
by Nancy Fusco Castaldo

FUN WITH MY 5 SENSES
Activities to Build Learning Readiness
by Sarah A. Williamson

Children's BOMC Main Selection
THE LITTLE HANDS ART BOOK
Exploring Arts & Crafts with 2- to 6-Year-Olds
by Judy Press

Parents' Choice Approved!
Early Childhood News Directors' Choice Award!
SHAPES, SIZES, & MORE SURPRISES!
A Little Hands Early Learning Book
by Mary Tomczyk

Parents' Choice Approved!
The Little Hands BIG FUN CRAFT Book
Creative Fun for 2- to 6-Year-Olds
by Judy Press

WILLIAMSON  KIDS CAN! BOOKS

The following *Kids Can!*® books for ages 4 to 10 are each 160–178 pages, fully illustrated, trade paper, 11 × 8½, $12.95 US.

HAND-PRINT ANIMAL ART
by Carolyn Carreiro

CUT-PAPER PLAY!
Dazzling Creations from Construction Paper
by Sandi Henry

VROOM! VROOM!
Making 'dozers, 'copters, trucks & more
by Judy Press

MAKING COOL CRAFTS & AWESOME ART!
A Kids' Treasure Trove of Fabulous Fun
by Roberta Gould

Children's BOMC Main Selection
BOREDOM BUSTERS! (Newly Revised)
The Curious Kids' Activity Book
by Avery Hart and Paul Mantell

American Bookseller Pick of the Lists
SUPER SCIENCE CONCOCTIONS
50 Mysterious Mixtures for Fabulous Fun
by Jill Frankel Hauser

Parents' Choice Gold Award Winner!
Parents Magazine Parents' Pick!
THE KIDS' NATURE BOOK (Newly Revised)
365 Indoor/Outdoor Activities and Experiences
by Susan Milord

Benjamin Franklin Best Multicultural Book Award Winner!
Parents' Choice Approved!
Skipping Stones Multicultural Honor Award Winner!
THE KIDS' MULTICULTURAL COOKBOOK
Food & Fun Around the World
by Deanna F. Cook

KIDS' COMPUTER CREATIONS
Using Your Computer for Art & Craft Fun
by Carol Sabbeth

Parents' Choice Approved!
Dr. Toy Vacation Favorites Award Winner!
KIDS GARDEN!
The Anytime, Anyplace Guide to Sowing & Growing Fun
by Avery Hart and Paul Mantell

Winner of the Oppenheim Toy Portfolio Best Book Award!
American Bookseller Pick of the Lists
THE KIDS' SCIENCE BOOK
Creative Experiences for Hands-On Fun
by Robert Hirschfeld and Nancy White

Parents' Choice Gold Award Winner!
American Bookseller Pick of the Lists
Winner of the Oppenheim Toy Portfolio Best Book Award!
THE KIDS' MULTICULTURAL ART BOOK
Art & Craft Experiences from Around the World
by Alexandra M. Terzian